Knowing History in Mexico

KNOWING HISTORY IN MEXICO

An Ethnography of Citizenship

TREVOR STACK

University of New Mexico Press
Albuquerque

© 2012 by the University of New Mexico Press
All rights reserved. Published 2012
Printed in the United States of America

First paperbound printing, 2013
Paperbound ISBN: 978-0-8263-5253-8

17 16 15 14 13   1 2 3 4 5

LIBRARY OF CONGRESS CATALOGING-IN-PUBLICATION DATA

Stack, Trevor, 1970–
Knowing history in Mexico : an ethnography of citizenship /
Trevor Stack.
p. cm.
Includes bibliographical references and index.
ISBN 978-0-8263-5252-1 (cloth : alk. paper) — ISBN 978-0-8263-5254-5 (electronic)
1. Historiography—Social aspects—Mexico—Tapalpa. 2. Citizenship—Social aspects—Mexico—Tapalpa. 3. Anthropology and history—Mexico—Tapalpa. 4. Tapalpa (Mexico)—Historiography. 5. Mexico—Historiography. I. Title.
F1391.T2185S73 2012
972—dc23
2012023754

TEXT DESIGNED AND COMPOSED BY CATHERINE LEONARDO
Composed in 10.25/13.5 Minion Pro Regular
Display type is Didot LT Std Headline

Contents

Maps, Illustrations, and Figures | vii

Introduction | xi

PART ONE: The Truth of History: An Anthropological Approach to History as Public Knowledge

CHAPTER ONE
What Is Historia? From Oral History and Memory Studies to the Anthropology of History | 3

CHAPTER TWO
The Past of History: Valuing a Public Kind of Truth | 19

PART TWO: Knowing History, Being Citizens of Towns

CHAPTER THREE
Knowing History, Having Cultura, Being Citizens | 33

CHAPTER FOUR
Skewing of History: Who Could Know History? | 47

CHAPTER FIVE
Juggling Rooting and Cultura: Cosmopolitan Citizens | 61

PART THREE: Other Histories: National History and the History of Virgins

CHAPTER SIX
Towns and Nations: Different Histories, Different Citizenships | 81

CHAPTER SEVEN
Histories of the Virgin: The Higher Ground of Secular History | 94

PART FOUR: Histories of History: Tracing History and Histories Back in Time

CHAPTER EIGHT
Shifts in History: How a History Changes over Time | 111

CHAPTER NINE
A Successful History: What Did Not Change | 125

CHAPTER TEN
The Success of History: How a Genre Prospers | 135

Epilogue: Citizenship Beyond the State? | 147

References | 151

Index | 161

Maps, Illustrations, and Figures

MAPS

Map of region covered by study — 8

ILLUSTRATIONS

ILLUSTRATION 1. View of Tapalpa's main street from the steps of the parish church looking toward the tower of the municipal presidency, 2005 — 5

ILLUSTRATION 2. My landlady Teresa with sisters, nieces, and nephews, chopping fruit to blend into yogurt in her kitchen, 2005 — 6

ILLUSTRATION 3. Cristero soldiers in the Sierra de Tapalpa, circa 1928 — 9

ILLUSTRATION 4. View of Atacco from the churchyard looking toward the primary school built on top of the original plaza, and the central block of houses, 2005 — 11

ILLUSTRATION 5. Municipal chronicler José Fajardo, giving the diploma in regional history class in Tapalpa, 2005 — 22

ILLUSTRATION 6. View of Atacco from the ruined chapel across the churchyard where church is in session, with the bandstand on the left that Federico's group had helped to build, and the central block of houses in the distance, 2005 — 38

ILLUSTRATION 7. El Tacamo, a rancho (village) in the hills to the west of Tapalpa, 2004 — 39

ILLUSTRATION 8. One of the grassy mounds of Pueblo Viejo, 2004 — 49

ILLUSTRATION 9.	Andrés contemplates the pool, now abandoned, in which (mainly wealthy) families from Atacco and Tapalpa once bathed on Sundays, 2005	50
ILLUSTRATION 10.	The novelist Juan Rulfo, 1966	64
ILLUSTRATION 11.	Selling "typical" sweets and drinks to weekenders in the portal of Tapalpa's plaza, 2004	65
ILLUSTRATION 12.	The late don Chilo, to whom weekenders were referred, in his cantina in Tapalpa, 2007	67
ILLUSTRATION 13.	Presentation of books on Tapalpa in the Hilton Hotel, Guadalajara, 2005	69
ILLUSTRATION 14.	Tapalpans chatting and watching a video of the Tapalpan festival in "La Coahuila" apartment, Concord, California, 1998	72
ILLUSTRATION 15.	Corner of the main square of Concord, California, 1998	73
ILLUSTRATION 16.	Mural in the entrance to Tapalpan municipal library, bearing faces of some hijos ilustres, 1999	76
ILLUSTRATION 17.	Independence Day parade in Tapalpa, 1999	83
ILLUSTRATION 18.	Revolution Day parade in Tapalpa, 1999	83
ILLUSTRATION 19.	Float in Independence Day parade in Tapalpa, 1999	87
ILLUSTRATION 20.	Procession in honor of the Virgin de Guadalupe in Tapalpa's patron festival, 1999	92
ILLUSTRATION 21.	Poster of the Virgin of Defense's annual visit to Tapalpa, 2004	96
ILLUSTRATION 22.	The Virgin of Defense in procession from Juanacatlán to Tapalpa for her annual visit, 2005	97
ILLUSTRATION 23.	Presentation of Martín González's history in the ex-parish church, now the municipal cultural forum, 2005	102

ILLUSTRATION 24. Tombs of the hacienda owner, Vidal Vizcaíno, buried in 1902 next to his first wife, in the Purisima Chapel, 2005 115

ILLUSTRATION 25. Vidal Vizcaíno's son contemplates the Hacienda de Buenavista in ruins before its demolition in the 1960s 121

ILLUSTRATION 26. View of the location of the old Hacienda de Buenavista from La Villa bar in the corner of Tapalpa's plaza, 2005 121

ILLUSTRATION 27. A cart, hauled by oxen, bearing the name Hacienda de Buenavista, 1999 122

ILLUSTRATION 28. The municipal council marching in the Independence Day parade in Talapa, 1999 127

ILLUSTRATION 29. Visitors being shown around an old house, run by a local historical association, in the vicinity of Concord, California, 2008 142

FIGURES

FIGURE 1. Ethnicity in Tapalpa's history in the 1879 survey 118

FIGURE 2. Ethnicity in Tapalpa's history as told in 1992–2005 118

FIGURE 3. Dominant view of Mexican society in the nineteenth century 118

FIGURE 4. Dominant view of Mexican society after the Revolution 118

Introduction

The British actor Stephen Fry launched a recent campaign called History Matters by noting that "historians, more than any other class, spend a great deal of time justifying their trade." He goes on to note that many feel that history has fallen victim to "a new and bewildering contempt for the past," or has been besieged by imperial guilt, until it turns into "one long, groveling apology." Then Fry changes tack: "Against this we measure the exponential growth in the public appetite for history." History has never had it so good—history books, TV channels and programs, blockbuster films, re-enactments, museums, websites, magazines, and so on.

What is history? And why do people find it interesting? This book takes those questions to Mexico, where I spent the best part of five years listening to conversations, attending events, and reading leaflets, newspaper articles, and books. But I had begun asking questions of history before going to Mexico, during my undergraduate studies in history at the University of Oxford; or even earlier, during history classes at school in Scotland. My research in Mexico led me in turn to the University of Pennsylvania, where I completed a PhD in anthropology but also took history courses. I take note of the differences in ideas of history in all those places, including at Oxford and the University of Pennsylvania, but I end up claiming that there was much in common in Scotland and Mexico, and at Oxford and the University of Pennsylvania. Indeed, the editors of a special issue of the journal *Public Culture*, with the suggestive title "The Public Life of History," reach a similar conclusion to that of Stephen Fry. Academic historians may be on the defensive, they argue, but public history is thriving (Attwood et al. 2008). My doctoral research also took me to California, where I looked at ideas of history among Mexican migrants and found quite similar ideas among Anglo-Californians.

Of all the things I could say about history in Mexico, I focus on one thing. My Mexican informants felt that knowing history could give a person public status or authority; it could help to make him or her stand out as a good or eminent citizen. That is the focus of this book and the main task is to explain why. Knowing history seemed to make for good citizens, but what was it about history that did so? What was involved in knowing history and who was good at it? And what did people gain from being good citizens?

It is not only in Mexico that history is linked to citizenship. The British historian John Tosh (2008) writes that history has been paired many times with citizenship, over the centuries and across continents, even if the nature of the link has varied considerably. Not only is history in the curriculum of schools across the world, but applicants for U.S. citizenship take an exam that includes questions about American history; the British government has moved in a similar direction, and includes history in the book that it publishes for citizenship applicants (The Home Office-Life in the UK Advisory Group 2007). Governments believe that historical knowledge is a good index of the potential of both natives and immigrants to be good citizens. Governments have tended to see history as a source of national pride and integration; others such as Tosh believe that nurturing "historical thinking" could make for a more critical citizenry (Tosh 6).

Much has been written already about national history and citizenship; the focus of this book is instead on the history and citizenship of towns and cities. I observed in Mexico that people talked (and wrote) of their towns' histories and not just of Mexico's history; they also had a strong sense of being citizens of their towns and cities as well as of their country. I will suggest that urban history and citizenship had a stronger presence in Mexico than in the United Kingdom. However, scholars have found varieties of urban citizenship elsewhere in recent years (Holston and Appadurai 1999; Sassen 2002; Isin 2007). Fewer scholars have written of urban history, but the history of towns and cities that I describe was not unlike the Colombian local *historia* described by Nancy Appelbaum (2003), the German *Heimatgeschichte* described by John Eidson (2005), and the *histoire de ville* of the Zairean intellectual Tshibumba by Johannes Fabian (1990). I found in recent fieldwork in California that most towns and cities had their own historical association and, when I asked about citizenship, several informants spoke of their relationship to their town or city.

This is perhaps an irreverent book. I treat history as one kind of knowledge among many others, rather than setting it on a pedestal. I compare history not just to legend, an obvious comparison, but also to gossip—and some will find that odd. Instead of focusing on academic historians, I talked to as many different kinds of people as I could manage in and around that region of Mexico, and I will cite bricklayers, priests, teachers, politicians, peasant farmers, lawyers, laborers, and migrants, as well as drawing on a talk by the famous novelist Juan Rulfo. I resist the idea that history is intrinsically interesting or valuable—that one simply must know the past in order to understand the present. Indeed, I reflect on the very idea of "the past" that we often take for granted as the object of history.

But if my book is irreverent, I do not mean to dismiss history. Nor do I dismiss citizenship, for that matter. Even if it did not always hold their attention, as we will see, my Mexican informants took history seriously because it was a serious kind of knowledge, one that drew on evidence to assemble truthful accounts. It was a public kind of knowledge, one fit for public consumption. Rather than agree or disagree with that, I concentrate on showing how history was produced, what people did with it, who gained authority from it, and why they considered it fit for public consumption. As it happens, I share Stephen Fry's optimism and I end the book by treating history as a success story, not least because history adapts itself to the times.

I have kept the book short in the hope of living up to the Mexican maxim: "the good when brief is twice as good." It is short because I have left much of the academic debate to four of my published articles, which develop the implications of my research for understanding:

- history and memory, although I note in the first chapter my discomfort with the memory literature of the last three decades, much of it inspired by Maurice Halbwachs (1980), and my preference for the work of scholars who examine history as a particular kind of knowledge, including anthropologists such as John Davis (1989) and Johannes Fabian (1990), poststructuralist and postcolonial historians such as Michel de Certeau (1988) and Dipesh Chakrabarty (1992), and literary critics such as Hayden White (1973, 1987);

- genres of speech or writing, of which history is just one example, drawing on the work of linguistic anthropologists such as William Hanks (1987), Charles L. Briggs (1992), Keith Basso (1996), and Jan Blommaert (2004), most of them inspired by the literary critic Mikhail Bakhtin (1986);

- citizenship, especially the tension between belonging to a place and being cosmopolitan, as studied by Kwame Anthony Appiah (1997), Derek Heater (1990), A. Linklater (1998), and Pnina Werbner (2006), although I take a broader approach to citizenship in a series of further writings (Gordon and Stack 2007; Stack 2012);

- the urban and its relation to the national, including not just the literature on contemporary urban citizenship that I have mentioned but also the cultural history of Latin America's urban cosmopolitan tradition, studied by Angel Rama (1996), Richard L. Kagan (1995), and Setha M. Low (1993) and the study of contemporary urban traditions, including the work in Mexico of Robert Redfield (1941) and John Walton (1984).

Although I have abbreviated my treatment of such debates, I am grateful to the publishers for giving permission to reproduce other passages from the following articles: "The Skewing of History in Mexico," in *American Ethnologist* 36 (3) 2006; "A Higher Ground: The Secular Knowledge of Objects of Religious Devotion" in *Religion and the Secular: Historical and Colonial Contexts*, ed. Timothy Fitzgerald (London: Equinox Publishing Ltd., 2007); "Rooting and *Cultura* in West Mexico," in *Bulletin of Latin American Research* 27 (2) 2007; "Trajectories of Culture in West Mexico," in *History and Anthropology* (2012, forthcoming).

One limitation of my study is that I focus mainly on smaller towns rather than cities, although I do say something of the metropolis Guadalajara, close to my research site in Mexico, as well as the smaller city of Concord, California, home to many of the migrants that I studied. That is partly because my project took shape as I was doing research in a small Mexican town, but small towns are good places to look at the border between urban and rural, and I have some sympathy with the idea that anthropologists turn up big issues in small places. A second limitation is that I dwell on the similarities of my findings in west Mexico to other regions, in and beyond Mexico, rather than on the cultural and historical particularities of the region. For example, scholars have written of the weight of conservative Catholicism in west Mexico that gave rise to the Cristero rebellion with which my study begins (Butler 2005; González y González 1968; Zárate Hernández 1997; Meyer 1971). I do make mention of the peculiarities—conceding, for example, that people objected to triumphalist accounts of the Mexican Revolution—but I have preferred to draw out the broader relevance at the expense of the particular. A third limitation of the book is that I focus on how people are ranked in terms of local and cosmopolitan knowledge as well as of urbanity and ethnicity, but give less explicit attention to gender and social class, salient though they are.

I am enormously grateful to my hosts in Mexico, especially the Gómez family in Tapalpa and the Rodríguez Figueroa family in Zamora, as well as for the support of my wife, Sara. My research and studies were funded in different stages by the British Academy, Carnegie Trust, CONACyT, Royal Anthropological Institute, Thouron Award, and the Universities of Pennsylvania and Aberdeen. I would like to thank Robey Callahan, Nancy Farriss, Douglas Massey, Matt Tomlinson, Greg Urban, and the many others that have read and commented on the manuscript. I am also grateful to Elizabeth Albright at University of New Mexico Press, Monique Nuijten, and to an anonymous reviewer. Perhaps the greatest intellectual debts I owe to Angel Villa in Atacco, who better than anyone articulated the sense of history that I outline in the book, and to Andrew Roth Seneff of El Colegio de Michoacán, who attended my very first presentation on the topic in 1993 and who has since then never failed to inspire and challenge me.

Sadly, the Sierra de Tapalpa has seen its share of the violence of recent years and I write in memoriam of two good friends, Alfonso Muñoz and Beto Hernández.

PART ONE

THE TRUTH OF HISTORY

An Anthropological Approach
to History
as Public Knowledge

CHAPTER ONE

What Is Historia?

From Oral History and Memory Studies
to the Anthropology of History

This book looks at ideas about history in Mexico. My interest in historical knowledge began long before I went to Mexico for the first time in 1991. I enjoyed history classes in a Scottish school and went on to study the subject at Oxford, before traveling to Mexico with the idea of doing my own research. I registered as a visiting student at El Colegio de Michoacán, a postgraduate research center in the provincial city of Zamora in the western state of Michoacán. While at the Colegio, I became especially interested in the 1920s Cristero rebellion, in which Catholic peasants, mainly in west Mexico, had rebelled against the government just established on the back of the Mexican Revolution (1910–1917). I was also struck by a book written by one of the Colegio's founders, Luis González y González: a "microhistory" of his hometown, written in 1968 and reprinted and translated several times since then. After six months at the Colegio, I had the idea of writing a microhistory of the Cristero rebellion. It seemed like a project that I could complete quickly, before continuing my travels or returning to Britain.

Things did not turn out so simply and I ended up asking rather more ambitious questions. What is history? What do different people find interesting in history? What value do they see in it, and what do they get from history? And what does it mean to say that places have their history?

I first went to Tapalpa in April 1992 as a tourist. Tapalpa was a small town that I reached from Zamora by traveling first out of the state of Michoacán to Mexico's second-largest city, Guadalajara, which was the state capital of Jalisco; from there, Tapalpa was a three-hour bus journey to the south. My parents were visiting and *The Rough Guide to Mexico* recommended the "highland village" of Tapalpa as a place to visit from Guadalajara. That first night in Tapalpa, I talked to a young bartender, Martín, who had much to say about the town's history, including the Cristero rebellion. He was from northern Mexico and had only lived in the town for a couple of years, but he explained that he had read about it in the life-long diary of a friend of his in Tapalpa, a man 114-years-old. I was intrigued enough about the diary to return to Tapalpa two weeks later. I kept visiting Martín to ask to read that diary, but he never did hand it over. Some six months after that, I interviewed the old man himself. Not only did it turn out that don Chico was only seventy-five years old; when I asked whether he had ever kept a diary, he laughed and said he had never written anything in his life.

Although my research had begun with a red herring, I found myself settling into Tapalpa anyway. The town had a resident population of around six thousand. But it felt much fuller during the weekends and summer holidays, when thousands of weekenders visited, mainly from Guadalajara. Together with the town's quaintness, an attraction was the alpine scenery of the Sierra de Tapalpa—red soil, pine forest—and the cool climate. Forestry, cattle ranching, and agriculture were still important to the Sierra, and over the years I heard a fair amount of talk about land—who owned it and what they did with it. However, many more men worked in the construction industry that was powered by weekenders' demand for country houses, both in Tapalpa itself and in the surrounding towns and villages.

Talk to the Elderly!

After a few days staying in hotels, I rented a room in the house of an eighty-year-old lady, doña Julia, the grandmother of my friend Carlos. On the wall of her dining room she had a portrait photo of herself with her twelve sons and daughters: four remained in Tapalpa, four were in Guadalajara, and the other four lived in the United States, where hundreds of Tapalpan men and women also worked, like so many other Mexicans. Doña Julia was very happy to talk of the Cristeros and of those times. Tragically, though, her

Illustration 1: View of Tapalpa's main street from the steps of the parish church looking toward the tower of the municipal presidency (2005). The steel framework is part of the second story being added to an old house that is now a hotel owned by an elite Guadalajaran family. It was later covered by a tiled roof to conform with the "rustic" image expected of Tapalpan architecture.

first memory, from 1917, was of her brother lying dead with a bullet lodged just above his mouth. Like many elderly Tapalpan residents she was born in a village, but her family had moved to the town during the violence of the 1910s and 1920s.

Carlos also introduced me to someone who would shape my research and color my life. Teresa was around forty-years-old and lived with her brother Jesús and her mother doña Agapita. I moved to their house after four months with doña Julia, and I have usually stayed there on subsequent visits ever since. More than an informant, Teresa turned into an interlocutor. She let me know what I could get away with. Jesús, by contrast, let most things pass him by, except for one day when I was complaining about the parish church. I said it was a monstrosity and pointed out that I had never seen a photo of the church. "Not so," piped up Jesús, "every Tapalpan family in Guadalajara has a photo of it on their walls."

Teresa took me to interview old people in the first few months of my stay in Tapalpa, introducing me to them as a historian. *Qué bonito*, I heard,

Illustration 2: My landlady, Teresa, with her sisters, nieces, and nephews, chopping fruit to blend into yogurt in her kitchen (2005).

over and over again. How nice or how pretty. I felt a little strange researching the history of a town so far from home, but very few residents thought anything of it. I interviewed a variety of men and women from fifty- to one-hundred-years-old. With some I got on especially well. One eighty-year-old lady invited Carlos and me to her house on several occasions. Doña Carmen had lived her life between Tapalpa and San Francisco, where her family had moved in the 1930s. Her family had been one of the wealthiest in Tapalpa, part of the "high society" of the early twentieth century. They were targeted by revolutionaries who attacked the town in the 1910s, and her husband was kidnapped by rebels shortly after their marriage in the 1930s. Doña Carmen had learned the piano as a girl, and still had a piano in her house. We took turns playing in the soirees that she liked to hold.

A few of the people that I interviewed were keenly interested in history, and we swapped notes. Soon after arriving, I was sent to talk to don Lupe Nava, a former municipal president known for his knowledge of history. Don Lupe advised me to forgo documents, which he said were few and far between, and to seek instead my own "criterion of truth from among the versions" of what the old people told me. I did come across some writings, beginning with the *Monograph of Tapalpa* that don Lupe had authored with the library staff in 1985 (Nava Lopez et al. 1985). I was given the *Monograph* in the Tapalpa library, when I asked about the town's history. But I took don Lupe's advice and spent most of the first months interviewing. Many other informants were, in contrast to don Lupe, lacking confidence in their knowledge. Some referred me back to don Lupe or others who, they said, could tell me more about history. A few others were suspicious and reticent, none more so than an ex-municipal president who suggested that I ask someone from outside his family, someone less partial about events during the twentieth century. A former Cristero soldier whom I tracked down back in Zamora first denied all knowledge of the rebellion, but half an hour later invited me into his house and gave me a detailed account of his role in the movement.

Tapalpa's History: First Attempt

I learned much about the Cristeros during those first few months in the Sierra, from talking to people who remembered those times and from reading books on the subject, including a pioneering three-volume academic work on the rebellion by the French historian Jean Meyer (1971). But I also did research on the centuries before the Cristero rebellion. Using the few written references that I did find, I produced a chronology of events stretching back to the sixteenth century and then I put together a narrative of sorts, helped by the work of a Guadalajara-based anthropologist, Guillermo de la Peña (1980, 1992). By the late nineteenth century, de la Peña explained, an oligarchy of landowners and industrialists dominated the whole region of southern Jalisco. A paper mill and an ironworks were built in the Sierra and a substantial workforce came to work in them. As the largest town in the Sierra, Tapalpa was the seat of the municipal government and its population grew quickly during the nineteenth century. There was talk of opening more schools, particularly in the towns, but relatively few children attended school. De la Peña argued that the industries of the Sierra were crippled in the 1890s by the building of a railway from Guadalajara to the Pacific Coast, which passed through the adjacent lowland valley (de la Peña 1980, 50–51). Curiously, those years were still remembered in the 1990s as a time of "high society," made up of the industrialists who settled in the town as well as a number of landowning families, who included doña Carmen's family—she was not the only señorita to have taken piano lessons.

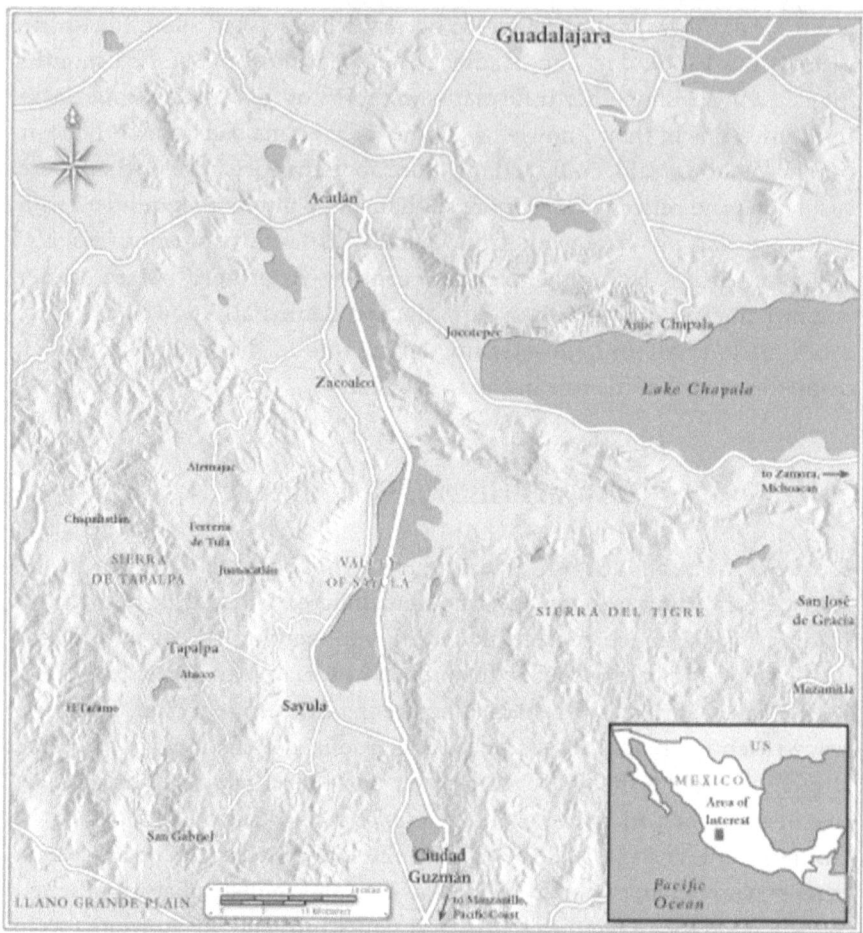

Map: Map of region covered by study (Gerry Krieg).

From around 1914, a series of attacks on Tapalpa and nearby towns, some of them linked to the rebellions elsewhere known as the Mexican Revolution, forced wealthy families such as doña Carmen's, to flee the Sierra. De la Peña argues that the national governments that followed the Revolution broke what was left of the "horizontal" regional oligarchy, which was replaced by a fragmented "vertical" order in which state and federal agencies, including the agrarian and education ministries, governed top-down through local brokers (de la Peña 1992; Zárate Hernández 1997, 170). National governments expropriated large landholdings across the nation, setting up peasant collectives called ejidos that were given use-rights to the lands, subject to management by the agrarian ministry. Locally, the largest landholder, the Hacienda de Buenavista, was broken up and its lands used to establish a number of ejidos, one of the first in Tapalpa's neighbor Atacco in 1929.

The Cristero rebellion began in 1926 in response to the anticlerical policies of the post-Revolutionary governments, as well as arguably to their top-down style of government of which land reform, carried out by the federal agrarian ministry with the support of troops, had the most impact locally. The rebellion spread across much of western Mexico, including the states of Jalisco and Michoacán, and I found that groups of Cristeros had camped in three places in the Sierra. The main camp was in a deep ravine in the hills to the west of town, near the village of El Tacamo (see illustrations 3 and 7). Many members of the extended family who lived in that ravine joined the rebellion, and two were officers of the Cristero Army. They had fought against the Mexican Army, which was stationed in Tapalpa, and against bands of agrarian activists, who were armed by the federal government. The parish priest hid with the rebels but did not fight. Those were hard times, many remembered. Tapalpa itself was attacked three times by the Cristero rebels. Much of the population chose to stay out of the conflict, although some Tapalpan women carried ammunition and arms to the rebels in the hills.

My study of the Cristero rebellion led me to inquire of the years that followed it. The population movement that began in the years of violence did not stop when peace was declared in 1929. The wealthy families that moved away from the region were followed during the course of the century by families of every socioeconomic level, many moving to lowland cities like Sayula and

Illustration 3: Cristero soldiers in the Sierra de Tapalpa, circa 1928 (photo courtesy of Sra. Consuelo de la Torre).

Ciudad Guzman as well as to Guadalajara. Migration to the United States was well under way by the 1940s, and accelerated rapidly from the 1980s on (Serrano 2002, 2006). But not all the movement was away from the region. Many moved to Tapalpa from the surrounding villages. Some families were forcibly resettled in Tapalpa by the government during the Cristero War in order to isolate the Cristeros; other better-off families moved to Tapalpa to replace the elite families that were leaving, competing to control municipal politics (and where possible to stymie land reform). Tapalpa also attracted weekenders in growing numbers from Guadalajara. An asphalt road up to Tapalpa from the Guadalajara-Pacific highway was completed in 1961, which is when weekend tourism became a significant source of income in the Sierra (Fernández 2004; Méndez 1989). Some weekenders settled in and around Tapalpa, including a growing number of retirees. The houses built for weekenders and visitors who stayed—over a thousand homes—have made the construction industry the primary source of work and have brought a further wave of workers to the Sierra. Tapalpa is, indeed, the only small town in the region whose population has increased in recent times.

Is History Too Bonito?

By the end of my first year in Tapalpa, I felt like I was getting somewhere with understanding the town's history. That earned me respect from Tapalpans and I began to hear that "it's those from elsewhere who know most about Tapalpa." Yet I still felt dissatisfied. I was asked one day, "Have the versions driven you crazy?" I was indeed not sure what to make of all the different accounts of the same events that I heard. To quote the old Spanish saying, *Cada quien cuenta la feria según cómo le fue* (People tell what happened according to how it went for them). Neither was I comfortable splicing together what I had read with some of the things that people told me. It was not just that they were different versions—people seemed to say one thing and write another.

Another thing that worried me was how Tapalpans responded to my project. What made history *bonito* for Tapalpans was, in part, that it was relatively innocuous; history was harmless enough to arouse curiosity rather than passion. Although they liked the idea of history, I found that their attention tended to drift after a few minutes to a topic of more immediate interest. I wondered if Tapalpa's history was worth months or even years of my life. I did find some people who were more interested, though. One was the aforementioned don Lupe, but I met another group of enthusiasts just down the road in the neighboring town of Atacco.

An Interesting History: Atacco Was the Town

I was sent to Atacco after the first few months in Tapalpa. Tapalpans suggested that I talk to elderly residents of Atacco, since, as they kept saying, Atacco was older than Tapalpa. Indeed, the one piece of history that most Tapalpans would volunteer was that Atacco used to be the pueblo (town), when Tapalpa was just a hacienda (estate)—the Hacienda de Buenavista. But then, they would continue, people from Atacco began to work on that hacienda, building their shacks around its great house, which used to stand on the corner of Tapalpa's plaza. So it was that Tapalpa became the town, they would conclude, even though Atacco was older. Since I was writing Tapalpa's history, however, they thought I should pay a visit to Atacco. Perhaps its elderly residents might know something of relevance.

Several months after I arrived in Tapalpa in 1992, a friend took me to visit his grandmother doña Julia in Atacco. It was a short though bumpy ride

Illustration 4: View of Atacco from the churchyard looking toward the primary school built on top of the original plaza, and the central block of houses (2005). Note the dirt ground of the churchyard.

along the two-mile dirt road to Atacco—the tarmac road ended in Tapalpa—but there was little traffic other than donkeys and bicycles. A series of small redbrick houses lined the entrance to Atacco, followed by a tree-lined and walled churchyard on the left-hand side. The small adobe church was faced across the dirt ground of the churchyard by the ruins of a smaller church. Opposite this were the primary school and a crumbling central block of larger adobe houses. Doña Julia lived around the back of the primary school, near a large stone-cased pool of water, in a small adobe house with an orchard. Like many elderly people in Tapalpa, she talked about the Cristero rebels. She also talked about her work for the wealthy Manzano family, who had later moved from Atacco to Tapalpa, leaving their crumbling houses behind.

While in Atacco, I was also taken to visit Federico, who was said to be interested in history, in his house two blocks behind the churchyard. Federico explained that he had founded a civic group five years earlier, which had undertaken various projects, including the restoration of the pool by doña Julia's house as well as literacy and hygiene campaigns. Another project was to cultivate the knowledge of Atacco's history among the townspeople. History was the focus of my first conversation with Federico. In fact, Federico began with what I had already heard in Tapalpa: Atacco used to be the town, when Tapalpa was just a hacienda. Federico spoke more vividly, however, of the Atacco that had been the town. He had learned from his father, for example, that people once came to Atacco from all over the region, and that a *camino real* (royal highway) used to pass through Atacco. "We've always had that idea," he insisted. The challenge was to turn that "idea" into proper history, worthy of a proper town.

As time went by, I was able to piece together some of Atacco's history, and to tie it into Tapalpa's history. At the beginning of the twentieth century, most residents of Atacco were landless laborers, since the community's lands were lost during the previous century. At least, there were no community lands when residents applied in 1921 for a land grant under the post-Revolutionary agrarian reform. That is clear from the agrarian ministry archive, which I first visited in 1994 (ASRA, Expediente Atacco). From my interviews, I learned that many residents had worked on the lands of three families who lived in the center of Atacco—one was the Manzano family mentioned by doña Julia. Most other families lived around the surrounding hillside in timber and thatch houses. I have mentioned that an ejido was established in Atacco in 1929 as part of the land reform. Some activists fought alongside federal troops against the Cristeros, who opposed the land reform. More than half the families in

Atacco became members of the ejido, receiving use rights to the lands expropriated from the Hacienda de Buenavista. The authorities in the town were the ejido committee, elected by its members (ejidatarios) every three years, and the municipal delegate, who was appointed by the municipal government in Tapalpa but who was always, until 1998, an ejidatario.

The ejido did not prosper, since ejidatarios lacked technical support and credit, often becoming indebted to the landowning families. Neither did the ejido have much influence on the municipal government in Tapalpa, which was controlled by the same landowning families, including the Manzanos; they were one of the families who moved to Tapalpa to replace the old elites in municipal government. There was no significant investment in Atacco until the 1970s, when a federal commission in southern Jalisco briefly targeted the poorest rural communities (Zárate Hernández 1997, 179). Electricity was installed for the first time and a primary school was also built, although this was placed without consultation directly on Atacco's plaza. Very few Atacco pupils went on to the secondary school in Tapalpa, but a small secondary school was later built in the center of Atacco. An area of land was also bought and divided into lots by a municipal president of Tapalpa, don Lupe—hence the red brick houses that lined the entrance road. However, streets and public facilities were in poor condition in the 1990s—several households still lacked electricity and drainage.

What Is *Historia*?

At the end of my first year of research, I gave a presentation at El Colegio de Michoacán in Zamora. Rather than offering a narrative of events, I decided to sketch out what my interviewees knew (and did not know) of Tapalpa's history, including *how* they knew what they knew. I distinguished, for example, between the "remembered past" and the "inherited past" of stories that they heard from their parents and grandparents.

Historians at the Colegio sent me to read the literature on oral history. Some of it resonated with my own experience in the Sierra. The oral historian Philippe Joutard (1986), for example, admitted of his research in the Cevennes region of France that:

> for a long time I did not worry whether this collective memory gave me information about historical reality . . . I was collecting

a testimony of another "reality" ... although I realized immediately that, in addition, this memory gave information about certain events.

A few oral historians such as Alessandro Portelli (1998) and Daniel James (2000) have managed to blend an account of both "realities," those of past and present (Thomson 2006). Other scholars, however, seemed merely to lament that "collective memory" was disappearing. The Italian sociologist Franco Ferrarotti (1990) regretted that people no longer partook of the "cauldron" of gossip and stories; the French historian Pierre Nora (1989) claimed that our collective memory is now concentrated in sites such as monuments where once it was the very medium of our lives. I discuss later the complaint of the famous novelist Juan Rulfo, born in the southern foothills of the Sierra, that the loss of historical knowledge in the region had undermined the sense of belonging, contributing to mass migration to the United States (Rulfo 1986, 15).

During a return visit to Britain in 1994, I discussed my research with various academics, including an eminent historian at Oxford. The historian listened patiently, frowned a little, and replied generously that it was very interesting but added, "it sounds a bit like anthropology." When we talked of a PhD in history, he felt that my project would only pass as history if I were to focus on how perceptions of history changed from, say, the 1940s to the 1960s. So I went to talk with an anthropologist, Michael Gilsenan, and explained that what really interested me were people's perceptions of the past. "Ah, he replied, *that*." Memory, a puzzle for oral historians, was all the rage in anthropology at the time. Anthropologists liked to claim, for example, that "history is a way of making identity" (Friedlander 1975, 837). Another commonplace was that history is made by the victors and not by the vanquished (e.g., Klor de Alva 1992, xii). Anthropologists celebrated the struggle of subjects to tell their own history, but added, knowingly, that people often "create" history rather than report "what actually happened." I will note below that most anthropologists sought to show how versions of history served to justify the interests of particular social groups.

I returned to the University of Oxford for a master's degree in social anthropology, followed by a PhD in anthropology at the University of Pennsylvania. But I became uncomfortable with the anthropological literature, too, and with it the broader field of memory studies. I realized that history was not just any old memory and that it would not do simply to identify different versions of it (or merely regret its passing). In fact, Tapalpans usually talked of history as something that one *knew* rather than remembered. History was, for them, a kind of knowledge. In thinking of my informants' talk of history as a kind of knowledge, I was influenced by linguistic anthropologists such as Keith Basso (1996), William Hanks (1987), and Jan Blommaert (2004), as well as by scholars focusing on local intellectuals, such as Nancy Appelbaum (2003), Steven Feierman (1990), and Florencia Mallon (1995). But lurking at the back of my mind was the title of a book that I had read years earlier at school: E. H. Carr's *What is History?* (1961). Carr's answer was less interesting to me than the question itself. What kind of knowledge was history? And what did it do for people? Later I added more questions: What did it mean for people to say that a town, such as Tapalpa or Atacco, had a history? And how did they relate their town's history to Mexico's history?

I claim that history is a kind of knowledge that was expected to bring authority to those who mastered it. For example, by mastering history Federico's group hoped to restore some confidence and pride in Atacco's residents. I show, however, that it was harder than it seemed to master history. Harnessing history's power was never easy, even if some people were better placed to produce good history. Federico's group found their own attempt at history wanting, as did many others. I ask, then, not just what authority was created in the knowing of history, but who was in a position to know that history in the first place.

I argue, too, that history was part of what made a town a town—a town was a place that had its history. So did nations, but I noticed that Tapalpans were reluctant to connect what they knew of Tapalpa's history to what they knew of Mexico's history. It was not that they preferred one to the other but simply that people made few connections between them.

Unfolding Research: Knowing History, Being Citizens

I returned from the University of Pennsylvania to Tapalpa in 1997 to complete research for my PhD in anthropology, and I made further visits in the summers of 2001, 2004, and 2005. Things changed, of course, between my first visit in 1992 and my visit in 2005. In Atacco, the ejido was further weakened by a 1992 reform to the Mexican Constitution that permitted ejidatarios to sell their use rights to ejido land. Some ejidatarios enjoyed a moment of prosperity when they sold their rights, usually to people from Tapalpa and from Guadalajara. Most then joined the ranks of those working outside Atacco, since there was little work in Atacco and few opportunities for commerce, which was limited to a small brick works, two or three food stands, and some tiny grocery stores. Few from Atacco had sufficient schooling to apply for clerical jobs in Tapalpa so most worked as manual laborers or as cooks, waiters or shop attendants. Many worked for the wealthier Tapalpan families, who had developed businesses, including a sawmill and several hotels, catering to large numbers of weekenders from Guadalajara. Others were employed by the larger companies that operated in the Sierra: mainly tourist operators such as the Tapalpa Country Club, owned by a wealthy Guadalajaran family, and agro-industrial companies such as those that grew potatoes. Many young women worked as domestic servants in Tapalpa or in Guadalajara. Men and women often migrated from Atacco to Guadalajara and some began to migrate to California, following Tapalpans, but in the 1990s there was still little evidence of returning dollars in Atacco.

In Tapalpa, the number of hotels and restaurants grew through the period, as more and more weekenders came from Guadalajara and elsewhere. Tapalpa was made a Pueblo Mágico (Magical Town) by the federal government in 2000, mainly as a result of the efforts of a businessman in Guadalajara with close links to the state government and part owner of a Tapalpan hotel. The status of Magical Town brought investment in the town's infrastructure and strengthened its urban image, and Tapalpa now looks quite different from how it looked in 1992. Despite the expansion of tourism, more and more Tapalpans migrated to work in Concord, California, especially after the downturn in the tourist industry caused by the 1994 financial collapse.

As for my research, I ended up talking to literally hundreds of people: young and old; rich and poor; educated and uneducated. I included weekenders and others who had settled in Tapalpa, as well as schoolteachers, bureaucrats, politicians, and academics. I conducted a sample-based survey of one hundred households in Tapalpa and Atacco in 1998, and inserted questions about history among all the survey questions concerning migration and economic experience. Beyond Tapalpa and Atacco, I visited several villages in the Sierra and did research in two other towns. Juanacatlán is known as an "Indian" town like Atacco, and is the home of a virgin adored by many across the Sierra; Atemajac is a quaint town like Tapalpa but does not receive anything like the number of weekenders. Beyond the Sierra, I asked questions and collected written histories in villages, towns, and cities scattered throughout Jalisco and Michoacán.

The question I asked people at every opportunity, was *¿Cuál es la historia de aquí?* (What is the history of here?) The question, which sounds more natural in Spanish, was deliberately ambiguous. Anthropologists often ask questions that informants may interpret in different ways—it is a way of asking several things at once. In analyzing the informants' response, the anthropologist must first decide how he or she has interpreted the question. In this case, a person's answers gave me clues about what kind of "here" might have a history; I found that most townspeople replied with a potted history, interpreting their town as the "here" rather than the region or nation. When I asked for the "history of here," I was also listening for what people considered "history" as opposed to any other kind of knowledge, as I discuss in the next chapter. In addition, I heard (or overheard) people say things as history, without my asking, even if in some cases it seemed they spoke of history because they identified me as a historian. Anthropologists always need to decide who they are themselves, in the sense of to whom their informants believe they are speaking, and I will note that many Tapalpans continued to identify me as a historian even when I tried to present myself as an anthropologist. Finally, in spite of don Lupe's advice and the red herring of don Chico's diary, I did eventually collect a number of handwritten, printed, and published histories—many of them histories of towns and cities—and gave as much attention to them. Although I had begun with oral histories, I came to realize that there was no clear divide between oral and written history, not least because I was often told things as history that people wanted me to publish in a book. Despite Alessandro Portelli's (1981) attention to the orality of oral history sources, oral history is not just oral narrative that is written down but, often, history that is told to be written.

Throughout the book, I examine what a variety of people said *of* history and said *as* history, as well as what people wrote of history and as history. I even look at what people said of what was written, and at what they wrote of what was said as history. I ask especially what kind of authority or status people gain from history; my main argument is that knowing history makes people seem like good citizens. Citizenship has followed hard on the heels of memory as a hot topic of academic and public debate. Most scholarly research has followed T. H. Marshall (2009 [1950]) in focusing on the rights that people can claim on national governments. I write of citizenship in a sense that is not often the focus of contemporary debates. Only recently have there been studies of the citizenship of towns and cities (Lazar 2007; Holston 2008); there have been similarly few recent studies of what makes for good or eminent citizens (Dagger 1997; Heater 1990).

Whereas I write of what Tapalpans called historia, I am less interested in how Tapalpans used the Spanish term *ciudadano*. When I say that knowing history made for good or eminent citizens, I am using the term to mean people who have acquired certain presence and standing in public life, a voice or authority in the town's affairs. I will mention at the end of the book, though, that in research that I have conducted since 2007, I have found that my informants, both in the Sierra and in the neighboring state of Michoacán, did speak of *buenos ciudadanos* (good citizens) in ways that were not dissimilar to my use of the term in this book.

CHAPTER TWO

The Past of History

Valuing a Public Kind of Truth

The Oxford historian had decided that my research was anthropology rather than history. It was well-meant advice, which I accepted by studying anthropology rather than history and doing an anthropology of history that focused on people's ideas of history. Looking back, though, the advice also revealed the historian's own idea of history. It was history if it dealt with what really happened, as opposed to how people perceived what really happened. But it might also be thought of as history if it considered how ideas of history changed from one moment in the past, such as the 1940s, to another moment in the past, such as the 1960s. That notion of the past was key to his concept of history. I begin this chapter by describing how Tapalpans distinguished history from other kinds of talk and writing. To begin with, I heard some contrast history to legend, which was about the past but not quite the same past. I was a little more surprised to hear others contrast history to gossip, which was found much more compelling than history. History was closer to the talk about land disputes that I heard from time to time, but I argue that Tapalpans felt history was over and done with in a way that land disputes were not.

Because it was about the past, people found history less exciting than, say, gossip about what was going on in present-day Tapalpa. They thought of the past as finished business and worried more about business that was not yet finished: family, friends, school, or work. I had been interested enough in history to study for a degree in the subject; few Tapalpans were moved to spend much time talking and writing history themselves. Yet history clearly had something going for it. Most Tapalpans could venture at least something about history; they also thought it important that I was there to write their town's history. In the second half of the chapter, I say that history had things to offer that other kinds of talk did not. History was valued because it produced a valued kind of truth, one that was fit for a public arena.

What in Fact Happened

Before returning to Oxford in 1995, I taught a class at the Tapalpa secondary school and spoke about my project. I took the opportunity to ask the pupils the question that I took from E. H. Carr: "What is history?" They replied that history was *lo que de hecho pasó* (what in fact happened). That was a broader definition of history than I was used to. Much of what I had heard and read at Oxford was about consequential matters, such as revolutions, reforms, and socioeconomic trends. I did hear of revolutions in Tapalpa, but I also heard about families, childhood, the way things used to be, others' misfortunes, town politics, the corruption of politicians, and so on. But although Tapalpans had a broad idea of what could potentially be history, they had a much narrower idea of what was obviously history. When I asked, "What is the history of here?" many people began by trying to say something about the town's founding. Others added something about a period of prosperity in the past, and about the revolutions that took place when the elderly townspeople were younger. That was it. Many Tapalpans referred me to someone who could tell me more about the town's history. Most often they referred me to don Lupe, the former municipal president. To get Tapalpans to say more, I usually had to encourage them and probe them a little. Once I did that the conversation would get going, and we could end up talking about almost anything, as long as it had "in fact happened."

Why did Tapalpans not volunteer more history? I have said that people did not find history particularly exciting. As a result, they did not often talk about history and had not heard much history either, so they did not have much to tell. Another reason is that figuring out "what in fact happened" was harder than it might seem, as I discuss in part III. To explain why

Tapalpans said little about history, though, I need to explain more precisely what Tapalpans understood by "history." I will begin by identifying what Tapalpans did *not* consider history.

I asked the same pupils about *leyendas* (legends) because I had heard the term used before, and I had also heard stories told as leyendas. For example, I had heard about a slab of stone in the hillside that opened into an underground city. The few who had entered had returned moments later to find that years had passed (or vice versa). Years later in northern California, some men from Atacco joked about the legend told of their town, that an eagle had come to rest on a boulder above the town, meaning that Mexico City was going to be founded there. The people drove the eagle away with stones. The men giggled, as they recalled the banter of their youth: those with protruding lips were said to have chased away the eagle, shhhhhh!

Legends were not history. The pupils said that legends, in contrast to history, were *lo que puede haber pasado* (what might have happened). In the following conversation during a religious festival in Atacco, Federico's brother Andrés was trying to interview Toni—a drunk from a nearby village—close to some grassy mounds said to contain pre-Hispanic relics:

T: Look, I'll tell you what is true, just beyond where we live, they took out some, right? That is what you're saying, right? We took out some figurines as big as this . . . that's what you mean, right?

A: What is that? Is it a legend or a history or something? What is there of truth in that?

T: It was when the world fell, came to an end, right? If you want, let's go to find some [figurines].

Andrés was not impressed by this obvious legend. Intriguing as it sounded, it would not make for history because it was not clear what truth there was in it. Truth often featured in talk about what history was and what it was not. The municipal chronicler, José Fajardo, was a great champion of the facts, rather like my early history teachers in Scotland—I recall one who exhorted us tirelessly to "isolate the facts!" Fajardo insisted in the regional history classes that he offered in Tapalpa in 2004–2005, that history was an account of the facts (*una relación de los hechos*). In one class, Fajardo queried why I asked anyone and everyone about history, rather than sticking to people who knew what they were talking about. One of his students followed up by asking whether I was interested in the "enigmas of the Rocks." He was referring to some huge rocks strewn across a valley near Tapalpa that had attracted all sorts of speculative accounts that were usually referred to as legends. Was my real concern, he implied, with the fantastic elaborations of legend rather than the bold truth of history?

I had heard Oxford historians worry about the nature of "facts" and about the truthfulness of history, although truth was still their goal and historians have produced tenacious defenses of history's truths in recent years (e.g. Appleby, Hunt, and Jacob 1994). I had also heard history contrasted to legend and myth. More strange to me was that Tapalpans also contrasted history with *chisme* (gossip). For example, my landlady Teresa accused me in 1998 of writing a book of gossip instead of history. She warned me against citing an elderly relative who, she said, was not a reliable source for my history, but she worried more generally that I was including members of her family. In other words, my book was gossip because it was not factual enough, but it was also gossip because it was intrusive in a way that history should not be.

I return to gossip in the next section, but an incident in the second year of my fieldwork pointed to yet another kind of talk. Don Jorge glared

Illustration 5: Municipal chronicler José Fajardo (with glasses), giving the diploma in regional history class in Tapalpa (2005).

down from the window from which he served the customers of his government store in Atacco. Federico had brought me to talk to don Jorge, who was endeavoring to recover Atacco's ancient lands. But don Jorge was suspicious—was I not interested in land for myself? "I'm not from here," I replied defensively, "I'm from Scotland." He replied, unperturbed, that an Italian had also come to get some land for himself. "But I'm a historian," I retorted smugly. I have noted that people kept saying that history was bonito. Instead, don Jorge scowled down from the store window, muttering something that sounded like *la historia es un guión para empadronar al pueblo*: literally, that history is a guide for polling the town. I cannot be sure exactly what he meant by "polling the town"—he was not an easy person to interview—but it was clear that he did not subscribe to the view that history was harmless.

To explain, don Jorge had in his possession a document that he described as the town's colonial land title. He insisted that this document proved that the community of Atacco was the rightful owner of the surrounding lands; Atacco's lands had been usurped by families from Atacco's neighbor Tapalpa. He derided as mere "squatters" the current landowners of the lands around Atacco, who were descendants of the same Tapalpa families. Don Jorge had been organizing groups of townspeople to claim back Atacco's lands, and his document was to serve as legal evidence for Atacco's right to those lands. Not everyone in Atacco agreed with him. Federico argued that don Jorge was mistaken in believing that his document was still valid as a legal land title. He maintained that the colonial government that had once issued colonial land titles no longer existed, and that the present government did not recognize such titles. Don Jorge was wasting his time and money—as well as other people's time and money.

Federico was still interested in the document, but as evidence for Atacco's history. Don Jorge's document had, according to Federico, become history. I have said that Federico saw history as one way of inspiring others to work together for the good of the town. He had obtained a photocopy of don Jorge's document, which he placed in Atacco's small library. Federico viewed his photocopy as a historical document that was valuable testimony to what Atacco had been—a document that was obsolete, to be sure, but one that was eminently fit for exhibition. That was presumably what bothered don Jorge. He doubted the innocence of history, its claim to be concerned solely with what was no longer at stake, which was what made history harmless for most people. Indeed, we might better translate the *pasó* of *lo que de hecho pasó* as "passed" rather than simply "happened." There was much talk of violent revolutions, and the blood seemed to spice up what was told as history. But people did not speak of the "history" of a bloody dispute that took place some thirty years ago, precisely because some of the protagonists were still alive. It was too relevant to make for good history.

The Value of History

Ironically, that cut from history much of what Tapalpans liked to talk about. Because it was past—no longer relevant—they found what was told as history rather insipid and talked only rarely about it. They did ask me about history, but I found that most were distracted by more immediate concerns, such as children, *telenovelas* (serial dramas), and politics, quickly losing interest in my answers. People also enjoyed being intrusive and personal in their gossip, and some enjoyed the enigmatic legends. Yet I still heard people say that Tapalpa had its history. Most could add that Atacco was older than Tapalpa. Then they would suggest I talk to someone who knew more, sure that someone must know Tapalpa's history, even if they did not. Every so often, one would say a little more, and a few, like don Lupe and José Fajardo, would hold forth.

So why did people talk about Tapalpa's history at all? What value did they see in it? That is the central question of this book, and I will only hint at an answer at this stage. Oxford historians made a living from history but no one in Tapalpa did. However, schools had done their best to persuade pupils that history was something worth knowing about, and I often heard people say that they should know more history in case their children were asked to write a project on Tapalpa. History was paraded on the streets, as we will see, as well as on the TV and in cinema. But it was not just that history had good press—people admired certain things about history. For example, Fajardo insisted in his classes that history was *el maestro de la vida* (life's teacher) and I have mentioned Rulfo's claim that history gave people rooting or belonging (Rulfo 1986, 15); Federico said the same of history in Atacco. Although Tapalpans pointed out critically that history was normally written by the victors and not the vanquished, a few mentioned as an exception the film *Braveheart*, which dramatized the struggle of the underdog Scots.

Above all, it was truth that gave history an advantage over legend and gossip. Legend was full of color and enigma but its truth was obscure— Andrés wanted to know whether Toni's comments about the clay figurines were history or legend. The truth of gossip was as questionable as legends, and Teresa's mother was once scornful when I talked with an old lady whom she considered no more than a gossip. I often heard people criticize each other's account of history, and also criticize mine. But they accepted, for the most part, the possibility that history might be true. Bonito did not mean that townspeople expected a fairy-tale history. On the contrary, I was expected to write a book that was grounded in *datos* (data or facts). When I first met the former municipal president, don Lupe, he advised that I should develop my own "criterion of truth" from among the versions of what had happened.

Part of what made possible the truth of history was its focus on the past. I have said that the events of history took place in a past that was removed from the present. That pastness made history suitable for public consumption. But pastness also made events seem independent of the person telling them, making it possible that a narrator could appear disinterested. Gossip, by contrast, was too full of the present. That also, incidentally, made history conservative. Once something was accepted as history, it became difficult to challenge. When Tapalpans offered a substantially different history, they were accused of inventing it, of letting their present interests influence their judgment. I have said that the municipal chronicler Fajardo was a great champion of the facts. In one class, he attacked a history written of a local Virgin (to which I return in part III) that bore the subtitle "A Historical Interpretation" (González 2002). History, Fajardo reminded us, is *una relación de los hechos* (an account of the facts)—not an interpretation. The author Martín González had, moreover, criticized a respectable parish priest's account of a 1920 ceremony in which the Virgin was "crowned" by the Archbishop. It was too radical, too obviously political, to meet Fajardo's measure of good history.

The pastness of history not only made it seem objective, it also made it fit for a public arena. Teresa valued history as a way of talking and writing that was suitable for a public audience. That was one reason why people talked about history. It was also why Teresa found it inappropriate that I asked her family for their accounts of history. Not only was it inappropriate behavior for a lodger; it made for bad history. What made history bonito was, as I have said, that it was harmless enough to arouse curiosity rather than passion. If history made for good public knowledge, unlike gossip and talk about land disputes, it was partly because the "past" of history was not any old past. It was a past that was objectively past but it was also comfortably past. The distance was what made it a public kind of past.

History was fit not only for public consumption but also for public debate, which was prized albeit more as an ideal than as reality; people regretted that history so often fell short of the ideal. I compare two conversations—one that was not about history and one that was—to show that history was expected to be fit for public debate and was judged by that standard. The conversation that was not about history took place, ironically, just before the start of one of Fajardo's history classes, in the local restaurant in which the classes were held. It included Fajardo himself, a lawyer who was from another town but lived in Tapalpa, and the restaurant owner Elena, who had lived some years in Tapalpa as a child and had returned in 2002 to open the hotel and later set up a group of local business people. The lawyer told us of an encounter several days before with three men in a café bar that sits on the corner of the square; they had accused Elena of something and the lawyer had responded, he told us, by saying that she was his friend and that they should not talk about her like that. If they had something to say, he had said, they should put it in writing, as had another member of Elena's group who circulated a text criticizing the group. Elena was curious to know what the men in La Villa had said about her but the lawyer refused to say. Elena, Fajardo, and the lawyer went on to discuss another group of men who got together each day to drink milk from the cow at a yard in Tapalpa—the lawyer referred to them as the *Unión de Viejas Argüenderas* (Union of Gossipy Old Women).

The lawyer's criticism of the bar gossip was echoed in the second conversation, which did focus on history. Juana, in her mid-twenties, had lived in Tapalpa for only ten years although one of her parents was from the town, and started taking Fajardo's diploma classes but then dropped out. When I asked her why, she said it was partly that she was only interested in Tapalpa's history, including the "origins and the truth of legends" such as the tales of tunnels running under the town that connected up various buildings, supposedly built during the Cristero rebellion in the 1920s. She began, then, by contrasting history and legend. Legends were intriguing but she was interested in distilling truth out of those legends. To talk about the truth of legends was to reflect critically on what one had heard from others, as well as to shed light on opaque topics, in this case the tunnels running under Tapalpa. History should also focus on the town itself rather than including other towns that were of little interest. Instead, she complained, the class covered all regions of the state and the pupils were often just asked to read aloud from the textbook, as a school class might. Juana concluded that the pupils drifted idly from one topic to another, and that some of the talk during class was just chisme, or *la plática particular de cada persona* (private talk). The lawyer had protested that one should not use someone's absence as an excuse to criticize them. Juana complained, in a similar vein, that the history pupils were talking about topics of interest only to a few, very likely about people they knew and she did not. Like the first conversation, then, Juana held up standards of public debate in order to accuse Fajardo's class of falling short. She criticized not history, which she valued, but bad history—as Fajardo had done himself. Good history was, like disagreements among groups in the public sphere, expected to hold to those standards, as public discourse.

Further Afield

I return in part II to the idea of debating the truth of history but I want to insist that I found Tapalpans' ideas of history familiar because they were similar to those I encountered in Scotland, at the University of Oxford, and at the University of Pennsylvania. I began the chapter by reflecting on the Oxford historian's advice to me in 1994. My research would not pass as history unless I was to focus on, say, perceptions of history from the 1940s to the 1960s. That sounded reasonable because I had heard at Oxford that academic historians do not write about the last thirty years—the dust has not yet settled. The past of history was, then, as past at Oxford as in Tapalpa. The history that I knew was also about public debating of one kind or another. Just as Fajardo got (or tried to get) his pupils to argue their points and cite evidence, I recalled another of my Scottish history teachers teaching us to write essays in which we set up an argument by quoting one historian, and then used another historian to shoot it down (as caricatured in the hit British play and film, *The History Boys* [Hytner 2006]). That schoolboy history was more exclusively written but Tapalpans thought of history as being *ultimately* written, even if it seldom found its way onto the page and its sources were in practice more often oral.*

History's separation of past and present has come under scrutiny but it has proved remarkably resilient. Many scholars have detected signs of the present in the past, and countless book and article titles include phrases like "the presence of the past" and "the past in the present." However, the

---

* Tapalpans often assured me that a book of Tapalpa's history existed but it proved as elusive as don Chico's diary.

presence of the past is only a surprise if we assume that the past could ever be distinguished from the present. The authors of a recent publication, "The Public Life of History," offer three ways of blurring the boundary between history's past and its present, but again seem reluctant to abandon the distinction. One way of blurring the boundary is by focusing on "historical wounds," by which they mean events that continue to hurt and so refuse to become past even as time passes, but which the authors still want to call "historical" even though their "truth is not always verifiable by historians" (Attwood et al. 2008, 1). Their examples include the genocides addressed by Truth and Reconciliation Commissions, as well as the stolen generations of Australian Aborigines. The second way of blurring past and present that they suggest is oral history:

> [it]s very practice brings the historian into closer proximity with the past. This has made it much harder for the professional historian to maintain the detachment the discipline has regarded as necessary for critical historical practice, and it has placed considerable pressure on historical objectivity. (Attwood 2008, 80–81)

Oral history is, then, a kind of Trojan Horse. I had started doing oral history in Tapalpa, following don Lupe's advice, and perhaps that was indeed what pushed me to reflect on the boundary between past and present. The authors suggest a third way of blurring past and present: intervening deliberately in debates about the present. In his contribution, the Mexican anthropologist and historian Claudio Lomnitz contrasts academic history with what he writes in his weekly Mexican newspaper column. Journalism, he explains, has different conventions to history. For one thing, Lomnitz borrows freely from other columnists and they borrow from him, but more importantly, he is also able in his column to make an "untimely intervention" in the present (Lomnitz 2008, 56). However, the authors of "The Public Life of History" still seem to give the past its place—they leave the truth of history in a past that can be narrated from the present, even if the boundaries sometimes get blurred. The editors in their introduction still distinguish "historical wounds" from full-fledged "historical truths"; Attwood recognizes that "historical objectivity" is threatened by oral history; Lomnitz admits that history written with an eye on the present is "certainly no longer a form of expression that is well attuned to a subtle reconstruction of the past" (Lomnitz 2008, 56). So the idea of the past remains compelling even for scholars who question it. It is so often conservative, despite the best efforts of critical historians. We have seen Fajardo heading off Martín González's rewriting of the Virgin's history by appealing to "what in fact happened." John Sayles gives another beautiful example in his film *Lone Star* (1996). Anglo teachers complain about the history classes offered by a local Latina teacher, who likes to stress the role of Hispanics in Texan history: "I don't mind about the culture," said one of them, "but you can't change who did what to whom."

Knowing History, Being Good Citizens

Because it was a valued kind of truth and one fit for and produced through a public arena, Tapalpans who knew their history, like don Lupe and Fajardo, got some credit for it even though no one made a living from it. It helped me, too. By the end of 1992, after interviewing more than fifty elderly people and spending many hours pouring over my notes, I found I could talk Tapalpa's history with some confidence. From that point on, my status in the town grew. Although I insisted later that I had converted to anthropology, many Tapalpans still prefer to think of me as a historian.

In part II, I say more about what Tapalpans got from history. I begin by saying that people who knew history were said to have "cultura." *Cultura* was all about the public spirit that was shown through an interest in history, and about the public arena in which people produced that history. History was the mark of a proper town rather than a village, since towns were places that had cultura. I describe the campaign of Federico's group to produce their town's history in order to make it seem more like a proper town. Being a proper town meant, among other things, having a public arena. I conclude that history made for good citizens—public-spirited individuals who boasted of cosmopolitan cultura. I show, too, that people were citizens of towns rather than villages, and that history was told of towns rather than villages. But I go on to note in the second chapter that knowing history was not so easy. Historical knowledge was valued partly because it was not an easy truth to get right. Juana was not impressed, as we have seen, with Fajardo's group reading aloud from a book of Jalisco's history. That also explains why most people had little to say about history.

It was partly that they lacked interest, as I have suggested, and they did not wish to offend people. But it was also because they lacked the confidence to say much about history. I end part II by showing that history was also a mark of rooting or belonging, and I will explore the relationship between having cultura and being rooted.

PART TWO

KNOWING HISTORY, BEING CITIZENS OF TOWNS

CHAPTER THREE

Knowing History, Having Cultura, Being Citizens

H istory is usually about place. Family history has grown in popularity and there are histories of organizations and of such phenomena as slavery, capitalism, and civilization. For the most part, though, what links us to the heroes of our histories is that they lived in the same place.

Not every place is deemed worthy of history, though. A nation is one kind of place that has history and the vast majority of academic histories are national. I return to nations later; I am concerned here with the history of towns and cities, which has mainly been told and written by nonacademics. Academic historians who do write the history of towns have sometimes classed their academic attempts as "microhistories" to distinguish them from the "local history" of amateurs; an example is the historian Luis González y González, who inspired my original project in Tapalpa. But I found that Tapalpans took my idea of writing their town's history quite seriously. When I inquired of the town's history, most people found something to say even if they then referred me to someone else who knew more.

I noticed later, however, that ranchos (villages) were not deemed as worthy of history as pueblos (towns). I asked the question, "What is the history of here?" in both towns and villages of the Sierra. The answer differed, of course, from one place to another, but it also differed from one *kind* of place to another. When I asked the question in Tapalpa, most people had a ready-made answer. They gave a kind of potted history of the town. I found the same was true of other towns in the Sierra. When I asked in villages, I found that people also attempted to answer the question, since in principle any place could have a history. However, they did not find much to say—there was no potted history to be told. Nor were they sure that anyone else would know more.

Why was history told of towns like Tapalpa, and not of villages? In other words, what was the link between history as a kind of knowledge, and towns and cities as a kind of place? Knowing history gave people something called cultura and towns were considered home to cultura. I will explain what Tapalpans meant by cultura and why they linked it to towns rather than villages, before going on to explain why they considered knowing history to be a sign of having cultura. I focus on the kind of evidence—especially archived documents—that people valued in debating history, following the approach of linguistic anthropologists like Keith Basso (1996), literary scholars like Hayden White (1973), and epistemologists such as Wallace Chafe (1986; see also Stack 2006).

I will conclude that having cultura was, in turn, a sign of a good or eminent citizen. The link of citizenship to towns and cities should not surprise us. The word "citizenship," both in English and in Spanish, resembles and derives etymologically from the word "city," as my informants sometimes pointed out. Scholars have used the term "urban citizenship" in observing that activists increasingly pitch their struggles in terms of people's "rights to the city" (Holston and Appadurai 1999). If citizenship is coming to focus on the city, it is returning home; people were urban citizens for many centuries before the rise of the nation-state (Gordon and Stack 2007; Herzog 2007; Sacks 2007; Barry 2000). I say later in the book, though, that the link between history, citizenship, and towns and cities varies from one country to another. In Britain, there is now less of a sense that towns and cities have a history, that they are home to civility, and that civility is in turn essential to what makes a citizen. Urban history and citizenship has survived in Mexico as part of the broad urban-cosmopolitan tradition, once termed the "lettered city," to which I return in part IV (Rama 1984).

Places That Have Cultura

Atacco Was the Town

I have said that I was sent to Atacco because I was told the old people might know more of Tapalpa's history. Atacco was more usually described as the most backward place on earth. In Tapalpa, the people of Atacco were known as *indios*, meaning poor, stubborn, and ignorant, or even *indiorantes*, a mocking amalgam of indio and ignorante. This view was picked up with remarkable speed by those who came to stay or live in Tapalpa. I talked to a young teacher from Guadalajara who was living in Tapalpa but teaching in the primary school in Atacco. She had originally thought of living with her husband in Atacco but ruled this out, listing a series of complaints about the place, including alcoholic parents, children working in the fields during school hours, and the lack of family planning, hygiene, and toilets. These she summed up as *atraso cultural* (literally, cultural backwardness). She found this particularly shocking given the closeness to Tapalpa and to the high-class tourist establishments in the vicinity.

I continued to make regular visits to Atacco, particularly from 1997 to 1999, and became friends with Federico and his brother Andrés, together with others in his group and in the town. Their group was one of several to appear in Atacco during the period; some were linked to political parties while others started life as church groups, combining study of the bible and social issues of the kind encouraged by the Catholic diocese of Ciudad Guzmán (inspired by liberation theology). Federico's group emerged out of these pastoral groups and its members gave catechism classes and helped to organize the religious festivals, for example by rehearsing dances for performance in those festivals. Indeed, Federico and his brother Andrés had grown up in Ciudad Guzman in the 1970s, although their parents were born in Atacco. Most members were between twenty-five and fifty-years-old in 1997, but none had more than secondary-level schooling. Federico, like many in the group, worked as an *albañil* (skilled worker in the construction and maintenance of buildings and streets). Several, including Federico, had also worked during the 1980s for a German-funded nongovernmental organization (NGO) that carried out projects in many Sierra communities, including Atacco. The group applied for and received the status of civil association in 1995, but it remained a largely informal group.

We saw in part I that Federico's group was in dispute with the group run by don Jorge, who had sought since the 1980s to "reclaim" lands in the vicinity in the name of an "indigenous community of Atacco." Federico complained that they were wasting people's time and money; their "colonial land title" was no longer valid because it was issued by a previous government. He also complained about the ejido—in fact, few members of the group were ejidatarios. For example, Andrés reported that the group received funding to install garden areas in the churchyard, but the ejido insisted they seek permission from them and the project lapsed. The group also criticized ejidatarios for their dependence on state handouts. The group received some funding for other projects, including from the state, but they still supplied the labor. Other projects, including a small bridge built on one of the entrance roads, were funded entirely by contributions of material, money, and labor.

Making Cultura at Home

Federico's group pitched their projects in a variety of ways. He himself sometimes took the neoliberal view that for projects to be successful people should have a personal stake in them. Others talked in terms of a community tradition that included cargo-holders assuming the responsibility for festivals and people playing their part in communal labor. They also distanced themselves from the state in more obvious ways. For example, they decided to name Atacco's streets after trees of the Sierra rather than after the nationalist heroes of every other Mexican town.

I focus here on one other way in which group members, particularly Federico's brother Andrés, pitched their activities. Andrés, who was thirty-six-years-old in 1997, also worked as an albañil. On many occasions over the years, Andrés talked of the importance of cultura, which has just as many meanings as the English term "culture," overlapping with some although not all of them. Just as I explained what Tapalpans understood as historia by showing how they distinguished it from gossip, legend, and legal discourse, I begin with what cultura, for Andrés and others, was not. On one occasion in 1998, he argued that the activities of the group were all about cultura rather than *política* (party politics). Andrés was proud of having participated in political parties, but he and others had often been sidelined because they were not members of the ejido. They also found that political parties, once elected, pursued their own agendas and interests or contented themselves with the salary and other pickings of office. This was what he meant by política; by contrast, cultura was the far-sighted pursuit of the public good. In branding their projects as cultura, Andrés drew attention to their lofty motives: they denied ambitions of financial rewards or political office; there were no strings, such as votes, attached to their projects; they chose projects of obvious benefit to the community, such as the sponsoring of festivals; they also chose projects of enduring significance, such as the building of a bandstand in the churchyard.

In distancing the group from política, Andrés was not rejecting the Mexican state. For example, the group played a part in organizing nationalist events such as the Independence Day celebrations (and the festival of the Virgin de Guadalupe). Group members also taught basic literacy and the secondary-level curriculum through the National Institute for Adult Education program and installed a small library, mainly with books donated by the Tapalpa municipal library—writing was important to cultura. They shared the concern of the Guadalajaran teacher about hygiene, alcoholism, and school attendance.

But Andrés did not see himself or his town as reliant on the state for cultura. The Mexican state had undertaken decades of "Cultural Missions" to emancipate Mexico's rural masses living in far-flung parts of its national territory (Lainé 1992). For Andrés, though, Atacco was no mere rural locality on the fringes of a nation, but a proper town in which cultura was already at home, even if it needed nurturing. That was important to the group's vision and strategy for the future. Cultura was one of several criteria—including population, size, and services—by which people distinguished pueblos from ranchos. When members of the group first petitioned for a rise in Atacco's civic status from municipal agency to municipal delegation in 1998, they were told that no one in Atacco could perform the civic duties. The Tapalpan municipal secretary was said to have complained that the people of Atacco lacked sufficient cultura to govern themselves. Federico's group was keen to make Atacco look more like a proper town. Key in this regard was an attempt to turn the churchyard into a civic plaza, hence the group's role in the building of a bandstand and the attempt to create garden areas in the churchyard (illustration 6).

Andrés felt that cultura gave the group room to maneuver beyond the política that surrounded the state. The group still made demands through política and it was open to collaborating with government agencies as well as NGOs. But it wanted to do so on its own terms. On the one hand, the group had worked reasonably well with a Tapalpa-based ecological NGO in

Illustration 6: View of Atacco from the ruined chapel across the churchyard where church is in session, with the bandstand on the left that Federico's group helped to build, and the central block of houses in the distance (2005).

restoring the swimming pool in Atacco's center. On the other hand, Andrés told me in 1997 that federal government workers had come to Atacco nine years earlier, drawn by reports of poverty and drunkenness. He proposed that the workers live among and get to know the people of Atacco, and he said that they never returned to the town.

How successful was the group's attempt to make cultura at home in Atacco? Not everyone felt that the group itself displayed cultura. Some criticized it for being too political, particularly for opposing the ejido and for supporting rival parties. The work of the group seemed to count for something, however. One member in his twenties, Beto, was elected municipal delegate in 1998, with Federico's brother Andrés as his deputy. It was the first time that a nonejidatario had been elected. In addition, in 1998 the municipal government raised the town to the status of municipal delegation; this was followed by other hints that the people of Atacco, or at least a few of them, were no longer considered entirely bereft of cultura. Federico was appointed to the Municipal Electoral Commission in 2000, a position of some responsibility. His wife was subsequently appointed deputy councilor of the municipal government and Federico himself was appointed civil registrar in 2000.

Places That Have Cultura

In a fine study of the neighboring Llano Grande Plain, anthropologist José Eduardo Zárate (1997, 180) observed of villages or ranchos that "the interest shown in reconstructing houses and buying electronic apparatus contrasts with their disinterest in common space." My informants in the Sierra had a similar view. What people called ranchos were, roughly speaking, settlements that consisted of clusters of houses surrounded by plots of land. They were inhabited by a few extended families, which were expected to compete among each other, each family in pursuit of its own interests. There was little sense of common interests or of public debate. What people called pueblos, on the other hand, were settlements consisting of neat lines of houses laid out along streets, which centered on a public square surrounded by public architecture, such as a church and civic administration. Pueblos were also inhabited by families and other groups that competed with one another, but the difference was that townspeople—or some of them—were able and willing to discuss their common interests in a public arena.

Illustration 7: El Tacamo, a rancho (village) in the hills to the west of Tapalpa (2004). It is difficult to photograph a rancho, precisely because it is not compact. The main Cristero camp of the 1920s was near El Tacamo and several of its residents joined the Cristeros' ranks.

Andrés described his group's activities as examples of cultura, meaning the far-sighted pursuit of the public good; those who had cultura were considered able to apprehend the public benefit that lay beyond the pettiness of interests. They had authority over those who lacked that ability. Indeed, the term was used most often in the negative, taking the form of "so-and-so lacks cultura." Those found lacking included peasants who sold their lands for short-term gain, individuals who threw trash out of car windows, migrants who forsook their civic duty for wage labor, citizens who traded their vote for promised favors, and politicians who were corrupted by personal or partisan interests. Ranchos were considered lacking in cultura and thus in people having the ability to apprehend the public good; the good of ranchos would be determined elsewhere.

Cultura was used not just to disqualify the residents of ranchos—to sideline them from municipal politics—but also to rank people within pueblos themselves. People were already ranked, in both ranchos and pueblos, in terms of whether or not they were "from here." For example, Arnoldo Zamora, the municipal president of Tapalpa from 1998 to 2000, was quick to reject the complaint of anyone that he considered "not from here." Those thought most obviously "from here"—especially the families that owned lands in the surrounding area and properties in Tapalpa's center—tended to play a prominent role in town politics. But some people were also considered to have more cultura than others. If rancheros were held to lack cultura entirely, in pueblos only a handful of individuals were expected to have a full measure of cultura, and it gave them authority over those others—not just in ranchos but in the town itself—who did not have cultura. For example, don Lupe, was often said to have cultura; he was also remembered as the most public-spirited municipial president that Tapalpa had ever had. Arnoldo Zamora, on the other hand, was not so highly regarded in Tapalpa, precisely because he was held by many to lack cultura.

Places That Have History

After their election as municipal delegates in Atacco, Beto and Andrés summoned representatives of each barrio, many of them members of the group, to discuss their plans in a meeting. Beto gave as an example the need to maintain the pool that they had restored, but he was interrupted by don Alfredo, an older member of the group.

Beto: I was explaining this to the president [of the Tapalpa municipal district that included Atacco] that here in Atacco, they say that, well, I don't know, but they say that Atacco means a place where there is water. So all the tourists who come to Tapalpa—there's a Green Guide, I don't know if anyone has seen it, it names the town of Atacco as the place where water is born [i.e., there is a spring], and says that it is the only place where there is a public pool where they can swim—and they arrive and see the pigsty, and leave laughing. When the tourist comes there is economic benefit for the town too.

Alfredo: I have always seen that this town is the oldest, to say it that way so you understand me. It's the oldest of Tapalpa and of all these towns around here. It's the most founded town. But we went there [to Tapalpa] and made it bigger, abandoning this town, and the governments we've had are always leaving it behind, behind, behind, and it remains in poverty. It has no future when it is the most *adelante* (prominent or ahead) of all.

Beto: So there are things here that are so important that perhaps you will not have noticed them. There's one important thing, which is the public restrooms . . .

Don Alfredo's little speech was laced with irony: they themselves were to blame for Tapalpa's eclipse of Atacco. His implication was clearly that *this* government—that of Beto and Andrés—must not turn its back on Atacco, but also that Atacco had once been a place with civic status. Beto, on this occasion, was keen to get back to the list of things to be done, including the public restrooms, but we have seen that Federico believed that Atacco had had an important past.

Some members of the group, including Federico, felt that history would help to substantiate the claim that Atacco had not always been a place of misery—and that there was something left to salvage. However, don Alfredo's speech was itself no more history than the narratives of eagles and of curses. History was something more specific: it was much harder to know history than merely to evoke a possible past. So how did the group understand history? I have already quoted part of the following attempt by Andrés to interrogate Toni about the grassy mounds, referred to as Pueblo Viejo (literally, Old Town), near his village.

Andrés: Here [Atacco] is older than there [Pueblo Viejo]?

Toni: Of course it is.

Andrés: But there are no remains here, and there are there.

Toni: Show them to me, you'll see.

Andrés: Here I can't show you anything because we went once to the INAH [National Institute of Anthropology and History], which is in charge of [cultural] patrimony, and I said to them, look, that wall [of the ruined chapel], I assure you that I can get people together and make a thousand meters of that kind of wall in a day. But that's not the case of you people of Pueblo Viejo, because Pueblo Viejo is still older.

Toni: Look, I'll tell you what is true. Just beyond where we live, they took out some . . . figurines as big as this. That's what you mean, right?

Andrés: What is that? Is it a legend or a history or something? What is there of truth in that?

Toni: It was when the world fell, came to an end, right? If you want, let's go to find some.

Andrés: Did your parents tell you that? Or have you learned it from life? . . .

Andrés: If you ask me about here, I'm going to tell you everything, am I not? But I asked you about there, Pueblo Viejo, where you were born and lived. It's your life, your history.

Toni: I was a worker in Guadalajara.

Andrés: Let's see if we can make a light history of Pueblo Viejo.

Toni: Well, if you want us to do it, we can do it.

Andrés was looking, then, for three types of evidence. First, he began by identifying the archaeological "remains" of Atacco. He did not seem too impressed by the figurines that Toni mentioned, although the group had also collected several clay figurines extracted from the soil around Atacco and displayed them in their library. His attention focused instead on the mounds in Pueblo Viejo that were said to be ancient. He contrasted the mounds with the ruins of the chapel opposite Atacco's church, which the group had wanted to demolish in order to extend the civic plaza. Andrés had argued that its simple adobe construction was not worth preserving—they could build walls like that in a day—but INAH had refused to give permission for its demolition. On other occasions Andrés, like Federico, made more of the remains of the royal highway that had passed through Atacco, which he seemed to consider a better index of the civic status of the place.

Second, Andrés was asking for a verbal account of those remains from Toni. The group had interviewed some elderly people and we carried out some interviews together. However, Federico complained in 1994 that the elderly people knew only *fábulas* (fables), while Andrés on this occasion asked whether Toni's account was leyenda (legend), a similar term. They were looking for something more authoritative. Moreover, Andrés seemed little interested in accounts that did not portray an urban, civilized Atacco. He had little to say, for example, about Toni's account of the world coming to an end. Nor was he impressed, on other occasions, with legends of an Atacco being cursed or chasing eagles away.

Third, Andrés did not refer to written documents, but the group had collected some documents in the library and often asked whether I had found any in libraries or archives elsewhere. Towns were expected to leave a paper trail—not only should records of the town accumulate in local archives, but the town should feature in documents far afield. The paper trail was a sign of a town's civic status. But access to those documents could be a problem, as we will see.

It was not just that Andrés was looking for a particular history—that was how he understood the genre of history, and others shared his way of understanding it. History was the knowledge of civic places, places that left certain kinds of traces and remains. A town was, in other words, a place of which history was known; towns, more obviously than ranchos, were places that had history. I have noted that in the Sierra people in ranchos found it difficult to answer the question, "What is the history of this place?" It was not surprising that Toni seemed more comfortable telling his life history, since

Pueblo Viejo, despite the name, was no longer a town if it ever had been, and Toni's own village was no more than that.

Andrés began the interview by inquiring about the remains of Atacco's civic past; he ended by proposing that they "make a light history." Although history rested on the traces or remains of the town's past, it was ultimately about what one made of those traces—the narratives or accounts that one produced. It was critical for Andrés that the group should play some role in producing such a history, not simply because he feared what others would make of Atacco's history, but because they should not have to get their history secondhand from others. That did not preclude others from making histories of Atacco. He did anticipate that others would be interested, just as he might inquire into the history of other towns. In the interview on the previous page, Andrés himself played the part of an outsider asking about the history of Pueblo Viejo. But townspeople should be able to play a role, at least, in producing their town's history; a town was a place *of* which history could be known, but it must also be a place *in* which history could be produced. That was Andrés's challenge to Toni: "I asked you about there, Pueblo Viejo, where you were born and lived. It's your life, your history.... Let's see if *we* can make a light history of Pueblo Viejo" (emphasis added).

Knowing History, Being Citizens

Andrés seemed to understand the knowing of history as a way of making cultura at home in Atacco. For example, the conversation in which Andrés distinguished between cultura and política turned easily to his interest in history. I found that many in Atacco and elsewhere shared his understanding of history and its relation to cultura, even if few took history quite as seriously as he did.

Why did people link knowing history to having cultura? First, history was something for which there was no immediate return. I have said that cultura was all about going beyond the immediate, and especially that of shortsighted private interest. There was little talk about making money or gaining political advantage from knowing history. On one occasion in 1993, I was lent a photocopy of don Jorge's document by a Tapalpan storekeeper, don Goyo, who said he had paid don Jorge for permission to make the photocopy. Although he asked me to make a second photocopy for him, don Goyo was anxious to stress that all he wanted was credit for providing the copy in my publications. That was public-spirited behavior, perhaps even a show of cultura. By contrast, I lent my photocopy to an elderly friend who later told me that her brother-in-law had shown an interest in the document, which alarmed her because she said he would want to use it for business purposes.

Second, Andrés linked knowing history to having cultura because of what we saw earlier, in part I. If the past of history was something out of the present and cultura was the ability to apprehend that which lay beyond the immediate, knowing the past was an obvious example of cultura.

Third, history was an example of how townspeople should behave. I have said that history must be fit for public consumption: it should be something that could be said publicly. As such, it was a mark of a particular kind of place and of a particular kind of person. History made Tapalpa and perhaps Atacco look like places with some kind of public arena, in which people could talk publicly about issues of common interest.

Finally, the debate was not just local. To "make a history" was to exchange truth with others in the wider world of cultura, such as myself. History was also linked to writing, both that of documents and of histories themselves. History meant being wired into a network of people who could, for example, cite evidence as they challenged others. History was, in other words, cosmopolitan knowledge, just as towns were cosmopolitan places.

If knowing history was a sign of cultura, having cultura was in turn a sign of a good citizen. Actually I heard the word "citizen" used in various ways during my research, and I have continued in more recent fieldwork to explore meanings of citizenship in Mexico. When I asked whether people with cultura tended to be better citizens, some but not all interviewees concurred. I have mentioned that the word "cultura" was also used in different ways, and several interviewees interpreted my question in terms of education rather than civility. Nevertheless, I found a strong correspondence between the qualities that made for good citizens, according to my interviewees, and the qualities that I have just mentioned, linking history to cultura. For example, when I asked Andrea, a middle-aged Tapalpan lady, about her virtues as a citizen, she replied:

> As a housewife I understand that I have to pay water, utilities, because I use them, and the more I contribute the more people are going to have them.... About going to talk with the municipal president, I know it's a right and a citizen's prerogative to go to ask for an appointment with him, but not to take a personal case for him to

solve. I would like to do more with social issues, issues that we have in common, than with personal ones. I would be moved more by the sense of community. That marks me out as a citizen.

Hers was just one of several different responses, but it is clearly resonant with the qualities that link history to cultura. Being a good citizen, for Andrea, was all about the common good that went beyond private interests. It was a public act—a formal appointment with the municipal president—and one in the public interest, just as paying taxes enabled other people to enjoy public services. That showed a kind of vision that went beyond the immediate.

People sometimes talked about themselves and others as *Mexican* citizens, and we have seen that Federico's group was keen to organize patriotic events in Atacco. But even though the group was happy to sponsor patriotic events, they were quick to assert their independence from the state, not least to distance themselves from the ejido members whom they considered too reliant on the state's favors. More broadly, I found in 2007 that my interviewees were reluctant to make their citizenship too dependent on the state. When I asked whether government had made them citizens, almost all denied that was the case. In addition, my informants often talked as if they were citizens of towns and cities, rather than just nations. When I asked what it meant to them to be citizens, many responded with examples of life in their town or city: driving considerately, recycling the trash, and so on. When I asked if they were citizens of Tapalpa as well as of Mexico, most agreed, even if they did not usually talk of themselves in those terms.

History offered a way of making cultura at home in the town, as well as claiming cultura for the group itself. Knowing history made for cultura, and cultura in turn made for good, enlightened citizens. In the rest of part II, I elaborate on the link between history, cultura, and citizenship. I have not said, for one thing, whether Federico's group was successful. They were not. History did have something to offer; don Lupe, Fajardo, and others were able to use the knowledge of history to gain authority as eminent citizens. But history was more difficult than it appeared, as I show in the next chapter. Moreover, history did not just make for cultura—it also made for rooting, which is the subject of chapter 5. If cultura was linked to citizenship as an ideal of civility, I will say that rooting was linked to a different aspect of citizenship—membership of a particular community.

CHAPTER FOUR

Skewing of History

Who Could Know History?

I heard a lot of people in Tapalpa and Atacco say they wanted to produce a history of their town but remarkably few ever got around to it. That was in part because it was trickier than it seemed. Federico's group was interested in history as part of their attempt to make cultura at home in Atacco—to make Atacco seem like more of a town. But they found it harder than expected to come up with a history, which led me to reflect on what was so difficult.

History was skewed. I do not just mean that it reflected the interests of elites, as many scholars have argued. I show in part IV that what was told as Tapalpa's history did indeed reflect elite interests, especially of Tapalpa's "old" families. However, I argue in this chapter, in the spirit of scholars like Walter Mignolo (2000), that history was skewed in a more fundamental way. Tapalpans understood history itself—the whole genre or way of talking and writing about history—in a way that favored those people who were in a position to make a good job of it. I was one of those people. By historia Tapalpans understood a kind of knowledge that fit their model of public debate, which I described in part I, and rested on the kinds of evidence that I described in the previous chapter, especially archived documents. I was in a reasonably strong position to produce the kind of history that they valued, because I had studied history at university and could travel and gain access to archives. I focus in the second half of the chapter on others who were well placed to produce good history, including don Lupe, Fajardo, and a regional chronicler Federico Munguía. I begin, though, by looking at the difficulties faced by Federico's group in Atacco in producing good history, even to their own satisfaction, and so to claim cultura and be recognized as good citizens. A brief comparison to Apache narratives of place will help to illustrate the way in which history is skewed, in the Sierra and in the world beyond (Stack 2006).

Not Good Business

In 1992, the group in Atacco had looked to history to help their hometown of Atacco recover from years of decline. Federico, Andrés, and others from the group began to record the talk of Atacco's old people, keeping the tapes in a small library together with a few photocopied documents. By 1995, Federico suspected that their quest for Atacco's history was not paying the expected dividends: "We've seen that history isn't good business," he said. Andrés persevered, but he likewise felt frustrated,

History was, for Federico's group and for others, a particular kind of knowledge. It was expected, as we have seen, to bring authority to those who mastered it. That was how Federico's group hoped to restore some confidence and pride in Atacco's residents. However, it was not easy to harness that power. The group could not simply "create" a history to make authority for themselves. They understood history as a genre that was to be mastered; they measured their own history against the criteria of that genre and found it wanting.

The history sought by Federico's group was, as we have seen, a history of place. Places can be objects both *of* which and *in* which something can be known. One implication is that something can be known of one place but not from within that place. That can happen when the evidence is lodged in other places, such as in distant archives, and when the know-how for turning that evidence into full-blown knowledge, such as narrative history, is also somewhere else.

Struggling with History

The group found Atacco's history difficult to come by. There were few if any architectural remains of the urban Atacco that they sought to recover.

The dusty churchyard in Atacco, where kids propped up tombstones to play soccer, stood in contrast to Tapalpa's paved and well-conserved plaza. While Tapalpa's old church was built of solid and permanent stone, Atacco's church was built of the all-too-ephemeral adobe with wooden timbers. It offered little in the way of civic status, past or present. Neither were there oral accounts that might help to convert the church into defensible history. What was sometimes said—that two missionaries had been killed and buried under the floorboards—was neither reliable nor a source of civic pride. The group had found no written documents that might help make something of the church.

A similar fate was met by the attempt to extract history from the grassy mounds of Pueblo Viejo (illustration 8). It was hard to link those mounds to Atacco since Pueblo Viejo was two or three miles away. In any case, there was little in terms of spoken testimony that might help—the drunkard Toni's account was hardly helpful. Nor was there any reference to the mounds in the written documents that the group had read. The group sometimes called the mounds *yácatas*, alluding to the pyramids found in the neighboring state of Michoacán and associated with the Tarascan Empire, centered on its urban capital of Tzintzuntzán. However, it was not easy to sustain the comparison of mounds with those carefully

Illustration 8: One of the grassy mounds of Pueblo Viejo, from which the group struggled to make history (2004).

excavated ruins. The group was left with just the glimmer of antiquity and no defensible history.

The group had recorded interviews with some elderly people. Few felt confident enough to say much when asked about history, perhaps because of their lack of schooling. Several, including doña Julia, did point to the central block of collapsing houses as remnants of the Atacco of their youth. The houses were in ruins, but had clearly been more impressive than other houses in the town. They also described an Atacco that still had its plaza and that was visited on Sundays by families from Tapalpa. That was a promising start. However, it was not clear to the group that this Atacco was the one that used to be the town. Andrés, at least, argued in 1998 that this was not the case. The Atacco of the old people's youth was dominated by wealthy families that had lived in the central block, including the Manzanos. Those families were not usually considered native to Atacco—some said that they had come from elsewhere and their lighter skin seemed to bear that out. They had shown little commitment to Atacco, abandoning it for Tapalpa around mid-century, leaving their houses to crumble away. Moreover, their relationship with the rest of the population had been that of wealthy, land-owning employers, much like the wealthy Tapalpan families for whom many of the group worked.

Illustration 9: Andrés contemplates the pool, now abandoned, in which (mainly wealthy) families from Atacco and Tapalpa once bathed on Sundays (2005).

The group had neither the time nor the money to travel and browse in archives, even if they got access in the first place. They found little imprint of the town in the few archives to which they did have access. Andrés complained that Atacco was hardly mentioned in the history that was shelved in Tapalpa's library, authored by don Lupe (Nava López et al. 1985). Yet he could only add that he had always heard that Atacco had been the town. They did remain optimistic that there were documents in other archives and libraries and Federico often asked about those that I had found in other places. When I brought documents, they made sure to photocopy and store them safely. Yet they found it difficult to make much of those documents—they never quite fit the bill. One recorded a legal dispute for which the indigenous community of Atacco was seeking one hundred pesos. Andrés quipped that the "people of then" were as broke as the "people of now," and it seemed they could make little else of that document.

I have also mentioned the "colonial land title" that was in the possession of don Jorge. The group had made a photocopy of the document and placed it in the library that they built. However, they found themselves unable to make much of the document—or at least to say anything authoritative about it. It was not an easy read: the script was obscure and their photocopy was out of sequence and fragmentary. Andrés mentioned the stellar lists of names and titles, including Charles V and the conquistador Pedro de Alvarado. There were some familiar places: Guadalajara, Mexico City, Castile, and some places in the vicinity. They could also make out a series of dates: 1530, 1710, 1867, and 1923. Those familiar references were all the more tantalizing: Had Pedro de Alvarado come to Atacco? The legal narrative itself—the "founding" of Atacco by Spanish officials, conquistadors, and missionaries—was unfamiliar to the group. This was not how Andrés and others understood the origins of their town. The group continued to make occasional reference to the document, but it did not make for any better history than the crumbling houses and the talk of the elderly.

Consequences

The group responded in various ways to the difficulties that they encountered in producing Atacco's history. Federico was ready to give up by 1995, but Andrés continued to ask questions about Atacco's history. They had not made ambitious promises, like publishing a book, so there was little sense of outright failure. Indeed, the quest for history might itself bear some fruits.

I have said that I was sent to Atacco to talk with elderly people. In 2002, Federico, although only middle-aged, was interviewed for an article on Atacco's history in a Tapalpan magazine, *A Corner of the Sierra*. However, that article stood in contrast to a second article in the same issue, culled from an interview with don Lupe. Don Lupe was cited as an author of that second article, while Federico was mentioned only as a source in the first. What Federico said was also interwoven with the arguments of "residents and researchers" that seemed to include don Lupe (Nava López 2002; Un rincón en la Sierra Tapalpa 2002).

It was quite easy to play down the significance of the group's failure to produce history. Achieving a historical account of Atacco was not the only project that ran into difficulties. For example, the group had attempted to resurrect an old *pastorela* (Nativity play), working with what the elderly remembered, but had given up after a year or two. Federico himself sounded confident that they could pursue other projects instead. There were other ways of showing off cultura: group members sometimes took pride in listing their achievements, such as the restoration of the pool and building of the bandstand. One could simply play down the importance of history. An old man quipped that the "past has passed, it has gone," while Beto made light of the irony that others cared more about Atacco's history.

That said, Federico, Andrés, and others were often self-conscious about their knowledge of Atacco's history. Not only were they concerned about what outsiders might say about Atacco—for example, that it was not so old after all—but they were also anxious about how to respond if others asked them about Atacco's history. Tapalpans might ask—Tapalpans had sent me to Atacco to inquire about history—and school pupils were often asked to write about local history. Weekenders were also expected to ask questions: Beto said that weekenders had asked him about Atacco's history while he was municipal delegate. His rather shamefaced solution was to learn by heart the two paragraphs on Atacco in the single-page "History of Tapalpa" that I had written for weekenders. Andrés was more frustrated than others by these difficulties. One night in 1999, after drinking together, he reeled off an anguished string of questions about Atacco's history that he had been unable to answer.

I mentioned that Atacco's civic status had been raised in 1998 from agency to delegation. In fact the new status turned out to be in name only and the municipal government in Tapalpa was still reluctant in 2007 to give the faculties and provide the facilities (such as office space) for a working municipal delegation in Atacco. Despite some improvement, I still found in 2007 that the stigma of being poor citizens—indiorantes, even—stuck to the town of Atacco.

Comparing

To give a clearer sense of what I mean by the skewing of history, I will contrast briefly how history is understood in the Sierra de Tapalpa with the Apache narratives of place beautifully described by the anthropologist Keith Basso (1996). Apache elders "stalk" Apache youths with stories—often of their ancestors' mistakes—that hint at the error of the youths' ways. For example, an old lady told the story of an Apache policeman who acted too much like a white man. Her granddaughter, wearing plastic rollers in her hair, felt that her grandmother was "stalking" her with that story. The stories are set in and linked to certain places in the Apache landscape. The ancestors' actions, including their mistakes, leave traces in those places and the moral of the story is read out of those traces. For example, many place-names are considered word-pictures made by the ancestors of the places bearing those names. The elders compare the present-day appearance of the place to the ancestor's word-picture and then they draw conclusions about the ancestor's experience in that place. There is no water at the place called "Snakes' Water," so an elder tells a story about how Apache abused the water at that place, and so, Snakes' Water dried up (13–17, 54–57).

Stories are told in Atacco, just as among the Apache, to illustrate the values that should guide one's life. Many are linked to the mistakes of ancestors and some are also linked to places. Don Alfredo's speech, recounted above, was a story about how the ancestors made the mistake of abandoning Atacco. The lesson to be learned was that one should not abandon one's town but, instead, cherish it. Place was, then, a cradle of values both in Atacco and among Apache. Wisdom—the knowledge of values—could be read out of the precipitates left by the experience of ancestors in a particular place. Moreover, the ability to read wisdom out of such traces created some kind of authority among Apache as well as in Atacco. The elder Nick Thompson's ability to tell stories about places seems to have given him authority among Apache. He was called to testify in court on behalf of Apache, for example, and told a story about a place that was involved in a land dispute (Basso 1996, 70).

Basso emphasizes that "the idea of compiling 'definitive accounts' is rejected out of hand" by Apache (Basso 1996, 32). The point of the stories was the lesson drawn from the traces, not the events that yielded such a lesson. Storytellers might be challenged on the grounds of their reading of Apache values, not on the grounds of past events. Federico's group, by contrast, was concerned precisely with achieving a "definitive account." History should ideally be the last word on the events that were narrated, not just on the values being conveyed. Don Alfredo's speech was not good history in that sense. On the one hand, his speech was unlikely to be challenged by others on the grounds of its moral content. By invoking the mistakes of Atacco's ancestors, he was able to speak as persuasively as the Apache elder Nick Thompson. On the other hand, don Alfredo did not give a persuasive "historical" account. It conveyed the values of cultura, but it was not a "definitive account" of the events themselves. That would not have been a problem for Apache: they simply made fun of the "definitive accounts" of Anglo-American historians (33–34). It was not always a problem in Atacco either: don Alfredo could make his moral argument in the meeting. But it was a problem for the group, whose concern was to produce history in a way that would not easily be challenged.

Who could pose such a challenge? Who might have the last word? Those who had better access to the evidence and the know-how to make something of that evidence. Apache knowledge was encrusted in the places of the Apache hills. The knowledge of history was lodged partly in places that were further removed, such as archives and academies. History was compelling and yet elusive. In theory, anyone could know history, just as anyone could have cultura. In practice, good history was understood in such a way as to leave the people of Atacco hedging.

Making Headway

Others in the Sierra did a better job of producing the history of towns, though, and some were really quite successful: the "old guard" of knowledgeable old men, who knew and respected each other; those who became municipal chroniclers (official or otherwise), and often enjoyed the patronage of state government; and the professionals, those who made a living from history. They became, some of them, the epitome of good citizens and enjoyed the public voice that it gave them.

The Old Guard

Don Lupe was one of the successful few. I was sent to him when I began to do history in 1992, and the library staff sent many others to see him. He had also helped the library staff write the *Monograph of Tapalpa*, and the Tapalpan magazine had published their interview with him on the town's history.

Don Lupe had the confidence to relate what he knew of Tapalpa's history to other histories that he had read. For example, he told me in 1992 that there must have been orchards in Atacco, explaining that there had been a small monastery there, and that he had read that the Franciscans generally planted orchards in the communities in their care. Andrés too made some reference to readings, but usually just to school textbooks and he did so less confidently. Unlike Andrés, don Lupe had easy access to archives and was familiar with them, not least because he was municipal president for three terms. In fact, as mentioned previously, don Lupe advised me not to waste time hunting for documents, which he said were few and far between. The Cristeros had burned the archives in 1928 and there were few records even after that. Instead, don Lupe had said I should talk to the elderly people and "form my own criterion of truth from among the versions"—he was confident enough to advise me to ignore the usual conventions of history. Don Lupe wrote nothing else, but his conversations about history were enjoyed by many Tapalpans. The assistant editor of *A Corner of the Sierra*, for example, said that he valued his interview with don Lupe more than all the others.

Don Lupe linked—in his person—history, cultura, and citizenship. I was sent to him for Tapalpa's history; he was known for his cultura, as I have mentioned. Most Tapalpans were suspicious of people who, like don Lupe, had been involved in politics, and sometimes complained of the lack of cultura of those in politics; I have mentioned that some made fun of Arnoldo, the municipal president from 1997 to 1999. Unusually, many Tapalpans did speak well of don Lupe's terms as president; he had the moral authority and presence that Arnoldo lacked.

Don Lupe also referred me to Alberto Arámbula, a lawyer who lived in Guadalajara but who was a native of Tapalpa. He owned a hotel near Tapalpa's main square, where he could be found on Sundays. Several mentioned Arámbula's knowledge of the town's history. I visited him in his hotel on two occasions and, like don Lupe, he set Tapalpa's history within a broader context that was gleaned from readings. He cited more documents than don Lupe, appropriately for a lawyer, and he was familiar with Guadalajara's archives. A transcript of a talk he had given was available in the town library. Arámbula, like don Lupe, insisted that oral sources were also important, and he recommended that I visit Atacco—he had landholdings adjacent to the town. I found that several Atacco people had talked about history with him. Beyond the Sierra, Arámbula had a public voice, although mainly in politics as a member of the state committee for the conservative National Action Party. He enjoyed a certain influence in Guadalajara, and had helped to get some Tapalpans into the University of Guadalajara. Many Tapalpans also went to him when they had legal problems.

Both don Lupe and Arámbula referred me to an article by a priest native to Tapalpa, Father Luis Méndez, who had died just before I arrived. Father Méndez lived in Guadalajara but had often returned to Tapalpa, and had the intention of writing a complete history of the town. He had published a history of the Virgin of Defense in 1948, which included some background information on Tapalpa and other towns, and completed an article on Tapalpa's history shortly before his death. As a priest in Guadalajara, Father Méndez had easy access to the ecclesiastical archives, which were a major source for regional history, and cited many sources that others have been unable to trace. For example, Arámbula spoke of a letter that Father Méndez had found between sealed pages in the parish archive, but I never found it in all the time that I spent in the archive.

Municipal Chroniclers

I first heard of the municipal chronicler José Fajardo in 1994. I was shown some articles that he had written in a regional newspaper, *El Sureño*, published in Sayula by Jaime Alvarez del Castillo, and in *El Informador*, one of the main Guadalajara newspapers, owned by Jaime's father and later inherited by his brother Carlos (who was part owner of the hotel on Tapalpa's plaza, shown in illustration 1). I found out later that Fajardo had been named municipal chronicler back in 1987, when the state governor decreed that every municipal district should have one. He was chosen because he was a friend of the municipal president at the time, he told me. Even by 1994, though, few people in Tapalpa seemed to know who Fajardo was. Perhaps this is why I was asked to represent Tapalpa at a meeting of chroniclers in Ciudad Guzmán in 1995, as part of a series organized and funded by officials from the Secretaría de Cultura. The meeting gave me an insight into the world of municipal chroniclers beyond Tapalpa. I felt out of place as a twenty-four-year-old Scot in a room of middle-aged and elderly people representing their own towns or cities. One of the chroniclers, Juan Vizcaíno, clearly projected more self-importance than the others, perhaps because he had published a few books, including a history of the Colima volcano's eruptions. When I suggested a round table on the Cristero rebellion, Vizcaíno responded that it would not be a good idea because the Cristeros were still controversial in the region; he recalled Cristeros being hung from lampposts all along the highway. The other chroniclers, however, were not so dismissive of my idea and were also accepting of my presence—a sign of history's cosmopolitan face, to which I return in the next chapter.

Fajardo eventually became important in the circuit of chroniclers in southern Jalisco, and deservedly so. My first impression of Fajardo's articles was that he owed a debt to Father Méndez, from whose 1989 article he had lifted whole sentences and even paragraphs. When I finally met Fajardo in 1999, I learned that he had studied for a diploma in regional history given by El Colegio de Jalisco. The experience had meant a great deal to him, and his writing in *El Informador* began to draw on a wider range of sources. By 2004, Fajardo was giving classes for the diploma in regional history in Tapalpa, as recounted in part I. My own experience of offering English classes in Tapalpa was that many people came for the first one or two but few returned. Fajardo had also lost students along the way, including Juana, who got bored by the gossip. But three students did persist with the classes and, by summer 2005, had gained considerable confidence in talking about history.

In 2005, I finally met the best-known chronicler of the region, Federico Munguía, in his house in Sayula. In fact, don Federico had never been officially named chronicler of Sayula, but the Tapalpa library staff had given me his regional history. I also found references to don Federico in the writings of academic historians and anthropologists, which was unusual. When I met with don Federico, he said he was always happy to meet with researchers and to share information with them. He had built up his own archive over the years. He explained that he was originally inspired by his father, who was a journalist, but that he himself was self-taught, spending his weekends in archives in Guadalajara. Rulfo had used his connections in the state capital to get don Federico's history published by the Culture Ministry in Guadalajara. Don Federico told me that he had always refused invitations to get involved in municipal politics, preferring instead to speak on politics from outside the system, both as a journalist and historian. Don Federico was the best example of someone who got cultura from history, and found a voice for himself as a result, writing about política but without dirtying his hands in it. He had founded a local newspaper in 1971 that, unusual for a local newspaper in west Mexico, was still publishing thirty-four years later. Don Federico was considered, in other words, very much an eminent citizen.

The Professionals

Many chroniclers had ties to academic historians, especially to those with an interest in local and regional history, and they often held them in high regard. But chroniclers and academics tended to keep their distance from each other.

I discussed in part I the "colonial land title" that don Jorge wanted to use to reclaim Atacco's lands and that Francisco preferred to use as a source for Atacco's history. Years later, the municipal chronicler Fajardo obtained a copy of the "colonial land title" from the Tapalpan storekeeper don Goyo. But Fajardo lost faith in it when he read the critique of the document from a Guadalajaran academic historian, Rodolfo Fernández. Fajardo read Fernández's critique out loud in one of his classes in 2005. Don Goyo, Fajardo noted, still insisted that the document was authentic, and he took some pleasure in noting that I had also referred to it in my 1994 history of a Tapalpan church (Stack 1994, 2). I had hedged my take on history though, by saying that "we have a document that *says* it is a colonial land title." Fajardo was not impressed by my defense. But it was the first time that I felt that someone had actually read don Jorge's document. Fernández was trained as an anthropologist, even though he was writing history. He wrote that the land title had probably been rewritten over the centuries, as peasant or indigenous groups had adapted it to their own ends. Fernández acknowledged that the document was of great interest, but he concluded that as a historical document it was not sufficient (Fernández 2004). Fajardo was struck by that argument. He echoed Rodolfo's admiration of the document, while agreeing with Rodolfo that it was not useful for history.* Fajardo had received his diploma from El Colegio de Jalisco, which had worked closely with municipal chroniclers and trained teachers throughout the state in regional history. The prime

---

* I had met Rodolfo at a party at another Guadalajara research center after he had finished his book on the colonial history of the region. I noted that I had some interest in the region's colonial history. Rodolfo replied, enthused, that he descended from the House of Avalos, who had governed the region from the sixteenth century. Whether because of his ancestry or the skewing of the sources that he used, Rodolfo's account was full of the Creole hand in the region's history.

mover at the Colegio de Jalisco was José María Muriá, whom I interviewed in 2005. Muriá had dedicated his life to the regional history of Jalisco, writing under the influence of the same historian, Luis González y González, whose work had inspired my interest in microhistory. Muriá had done well from history. Not only did he earn a living from it and the status that comes with directing a research institute, he agreed that his knowledge of history had made him an eminent citizen. In 2005 he had just become a member of the Zapopan municipal council in Guadalajara; I asked him whether he thought that being a historian had helped him, and he replied that that was precisely the reason why he had been nominated for the position.

Professional historians were often critical of chroniclers, even when they worked with them or drew from them. Muriá complained that most local historians or chroniclers were old-fashioned in their approach to history, and refused to go beyond the limits of their parishes. He noted that chroniclers all too often simply reproduced the documents that they found in the archives at their disposal, one after the other, in chronological order. When they reached the twentieth century, Muriá said, chroniclers had difficulty because there was so much more material available. At that point, chroniclers tended to structure their histories by the three-year terms of municipal presidents, including within each section what they considered the main incidents of the those years. That made for very boring history, he concluded; small wonder, he added, that children found history so unappealing.

I found that chroniclers were aware of the criticisms of academic historians, and they responded in various ways. Many were deferential and admitted their limitations, while making some effort to "improve" their histories. For example, Fajardo was sure to cover the whole state of Jalisco, rather than just a particular region, in the diploma classes that he offered in Tapalpa. He often referred to Muriá and others in glowing terms. Fajardo was far from the only chronicler to have ties to academic institutions. In the Sierra del Tigre to the east of Tapalpa, I found that the local chroniclers had close ties with Luis González y González, whose classic microhistory was on his hometown in the Sierra. Not all chroniclers, however, deferred to Muriá. Two accused him of drawing on the work of chroniclers without giving them credit for it. Others denied his charge that they failed to transcend the boundaries of their municipal district. The municipal chronicler of Chapala, for example, noted that his history covered the whole region of Lake Chapala, which included several municipal districts.

Adding Rooting *to the* Mix

I return to the skewing of history in part IV, when I note that skewing did not just give some people authority over others as good citizens—it allowed some people to shape what was told as history. For now, I continue to focus on the authority that people received from knowing history, which yielded not just cultura but also rooting or belonging.

CHAPTER FIVE

Juggling Rooting and Cultura

Cosmopolitan Citizens

History is not just about cultura—it is also about belonging. That is why immigrants in so many countries have to learn some history before they are granted citizenship. British history, for example, has been condensed into a short book that tells would-be citizens all they need to know about the subject (The Home Office-Life in the UK Advisory Group 2007). There were no formal tests for prospective citizens of Tapalpa, but Tapalpans still associated history with being "from here." Being "from here" had its benefits and outsiders complained of feeling excluded. Some outsiders tried to learn history, and I for one found that knowing the town's history made me accepted in a way that few others were. History is not just a way into citizenship, though. It is also a sign of commitment by those who are already citizens. Some felt that local history could generate the kind of commitment that would stop people from leaving town. Federico's group linked history to "rooting" because they felt that history would help people not abandon Atacco. People across west Mexico left the area a great deal of the time—mainly for cities like Guadalajara and for the United States. Many Tapalpans had worked in the United States at some point, which could offer them economic status but could also stigmatize them as rootless. I have mentioned that Rulfo—in a talk he gave in 1984 shortly before his death—also linked a lack of historical knowledge to the waves of northward emigration.

If history was linked to rooting as well as cultura, it was tricky to juggle them both. The Princeton philosopher Kwame Anthony Appiah has written of the "rooted cosmopolitan," exemplified by his Ghanaian father: "it was . . . as an Asante that [he] recognized and admired Cicero" (Appiah 1997, 638). Others who migrated could commit to their adopted homelands, in his case the United States, without betraying the places from which they had come. I have said that cultura had a cosmopolitan edge and that history likewise consisted of knowledge with a cosmopolitan twist—toward ways of knowing and through archives of documents in far-off places. I found that many in west Mexico aspired to the cosmopolitan horizons of cultura without losing commitment to the places in which they lived and dreamed, and that the history of towns offered one way to combine cultura and rooting. Few were as successful as Appiah and his father. Weekenders from Guadalajara hoped to find some knowledge of the past in Tapalpa, especially among the elderly people, who were rooted the most. They did not expect to find, in a mere pueblo, the full-fledged kind of history that is a sign of cultura. Even worse, Tapalpans who had migrated to California were felt to have lost their rooting without picking up cultura along the way. Tapalpans who stayed behind doubted that migrants could make any contribution to a history of Tapalpa. Instead, I found in my visits to California that migrants were the most interested of all in Tapalpa's history, anxious to show their commitment to the town.

Who could aspire to blend the virtues of rooting and cultura? One example was Rulfo himself, who had emigrated too, but to the world of Mexico City literati rather than to work in the fields, kitchens, and construction sites of California. His 1984 talk was organized by intellectuals from the region anxious to claim Rulfo as an "illustrious son" of the region. He was a fine example of a "rooted cosmopolitan" or, we might say, cosmopolitan citizen, who could balance commitment to a place or places with horizons that stretched far beyond. His talk and the discussion that followed was a wonderful balancing act of rooting and cultura. Fajardo and don Lupe were also cosmopolitan citizens, albeit of less stature; they, too, could juggle commitment to the town and access to the wider circuits of cultura (Stack 2007[b]).

Rooting and Knowledge of the Past

Rulfo was one of the many west Mexicans who looked down on emigrants. That is evident from his 1984 talk, given at the University of Colima, in the neighboring state of Colima. Rulfo was known for a book of short stories, *El Llano en Llamas* (1953), and a novel, *Pedro Páramo* (1955), which was considered among the greatest works of fiction in the Spanish language, but his lecture was about Colima's history. Following his talk, Rulfo was asked, "What is the point of history?" and he replied:

> It's what *arraiga* (roots) man to his land, it's what makes man stay and have love for the place where he lives. It's precisely the reason for which many have migrated to the US: the fact that they lack knowledge of their past and of the place where they live. The day that they know their ancestors, the day that they know that worthy men lived in those places where they live, the day that they know that this land has yielded fine examples of a living *cultura*, man becomes more rooted, puts more trust in his work and has awareness of the place where he lives (Rulfo 1986, 64, trans. by Trevor Stack).

Rulfo uses the term "cultura" for the archaeological remains that he discussed in his talk, but that is still resonant with the use that I described in the previous two chapters. What makes those archaeological remains cultura, we infer, is that the remains have endured over time, while becoming well known beyond the region. They have transcended the immediate, both in time and space. Note that Rulfo places this "living cultura," ironically, in the past and seems to consider few of the region's current residents to be capable of cultura. By acquiring some "knowledge of the past," they might gain some rooting, which would stop them from migrating to the United States. But what Rulfo means by "knowledge of the past" is something inferior to the "history" that he serves up in his lecture. He appears to mean anecdotal stories, memories of the elderly, or even the second-hand knowledge that comes from attending lectures, rather than the kind of "history" that is bolstered with archival evidence and packed with challenges to other historians. That full-fledged history was a sign not just of rooting but of cultura. It meant being wired into a network of people who could, for example, cite evidence as they challenged others. It was also something for which there was little

Illustration 10: The novelist Juan Rulfo
(photo courtesy of Ted Lyons, taken in 1966).

immediate return. History was, in other words, cosmopolitan knowledge. Rulfo, for his part, was considered very much a man of cultura.

Rooting was still important for Rulfo, and the same was true of Federico's group, who worried about Atacco's residents "abandoning" their town for Tapalpa. Federico, like Rulfo, seemed to feel that knowledge of the past might encourage people to stay rooted in Atacco. Rooting was also a way of ranking people. I often heard those who had not lived for long in Tapalpa complain of being sidelined because they were not "from here." It was said that Tapalpa municipal president Arnoldo Zamora refused to respond to those who were not from there. Other residents pointed out that Arnoldo himself grew up in a village near Tapalpa, not in the town itself, and that he was just borrowing the house of his brother, who had lived for years in California. After arriving in Tapalpa in 1992, moreover, I was sent to talk to old people in and around the center of Tapalpa. It was only later that I realized that they were not just old people, but were considered to be from "old" families; as such, they appeared to be the most obviously "from here." I will argue in part IV that those families were able to play a role in shaping what was told as Tapalpa's history.

But rooting alone made only for a certain kind of history. I have said that Tapalpans referred me to don Lupe, after giving me a potted history of the town; they expected don Lupe to provide me with the full-blown history that they felt unable to offer. Similarly, as we saw in chapter 3, Federico's group wanted more than just rooting, and Federico wanted to be thought of as more than just an informant on his town's history. Federico, like Rulfo, was clearly intent on producing proper history himself. He had interviewed old people in Atacco, probing their memory of old times, in order to turn those memories into proper history. Tapalpans were more sure, however, that someone such as don Lupe would actually know the town's history; many spoke confidently of an existing book on Tapalpa's history, although I never did find one. Tapalpans were also more confident that there was cultura in Tapalpa—that at least some Tapalpans had cultura. I argue in the next section, however, that not everyone saw Tapalpa in that light.

Weekenders' Views of Tapalpans: Rooting not Cultura

Weekenders from Guadalajara did hope to find some kind of knowledge of the past in Tapalpa, but did not expect to find full-fledged history. In other words, like Rulfo, they expected Tapalpans to show some kind of rooting but not cultura. I note that Tapalpans played up to this role—partly by producing idiosyncratic accounts of the past—although some found it difficult to live even the rooted lives expected of them. Meanwhile, some Guadalajarans tried to claim that they were rooted in Tapalpa, while claiming more cultura than other weekenders.

Tapalpa was visited by thousands of weekenders, mainly from Guadalajara, attracted in part by its image as a pueblo *típico* or typical small

Illustration 11: Selling "typical" sweets and drinks to weekenders in the portal of Tapalpa's plaza (2004).

town. Many city residents across Mexico, especially the bourgeois, like to "escape" to small towns on weekends, as well as to the beach resorts of Puerto Vallarta and Manzanillo. The term "típico" was used more generally for "customs" viewed as quaintly backward and for homemade products such as cheeses and alcoholic punches. Tapalpa was also enjoyed for its cobbled streets, red-tiled roofs, and whitewashed walls, many made from locally produced adobe brick (see illustration 1). The Tapalpa Country Club manager, Enrique, said in a conversation with the municipal tourism official, that Tapalpa was one of the best-preserved pueblos in Mexico. It was "like being in the nineteenth century," he said. There were, indeed, feature stories on Tapalpa in the national magazine of cultural tourism, *México desconocido* (Unknown Mexico).

History was not a priority for weekenders. During my fieldwork, I asked dozens of them—as well as tourism employers and employees—about history. The restaurant owner, Elena, said in 2004 that weekenders did sometimes ask about Tapalpa's history as well as about the history of the building itself. But the hostess said that they asked much more often about places to visit and about places to eat and drink. Most others in the tourist industry confirmed that only rarely did weekenders ask for Tapalpa's history. I argue that this was in part because of Tapalpa's tourist image. Weekenders came to Tapalpa for many reasons, but on the whole they came to relax. It was not a colonial city in the style of Guadalajara or Guanajuato, which weekenders visited with a list of sights to be seen. Some weekenders said that history was important, when I asked about it, but few expressed much interest. Tapalpa, pueblo típico, where urbanites spent weekends in the country, was not really about history. That is also reflected in an article written for American retirees in nearby Lake Chapala: the author feels the need to remind readers that "Tapalpa . . . has a rich and lengthy history one should be aware of while sipping the local beverages and inhaling nothing but fragrant wood smoke from local kitchens and chimeneas" (Tschida 1991).

Perhaps that was just as well, because few residents felt confident enough to relay much history. I have noted that residents were fairly sure that Tapalpa had its history and that someone such as don Lupe knew that history, but they usually only offered the potted history of how Tapalpa was founded. Several said, nevertheless, that they would like to know more—in case they were asked by weekenders. Elena was concerned to learn more about Tapalpa's history and the history of her restaurant. Many Tapalpans wanted to learn dates and names, which were absent from the stories they had heard from their grandparents. In the case of Atacco, even though weekenders did not often stop there, the deputy Beto had still memorized the single-page "History of Tapalpa" that I had written for weekenders.

Actually, I found that when weekenders did ask for history, they were seldom looking for specific dates and names or for the kind of history that they might find in Guadalajara. Their favorite historian was the *cantinero* don Chilo, who specialized in larger-than-life stories that lacked in cultura but had plenty of arraigo (although he also showed off a collection of photos of Tapalpan streets taken by Rulfo). Don Chilo's histories were of ghostly apparitions and of mysterious legends, as well as of stubborn caciques and recalcitrant rebels. They were a far cry from the formal public talks of municipal chroniclers. During an event at the Hilton Hotel in Guadalajara, in which four books on Tapalpa were officially launched, don Chilo was awarded a shield by the Tapalpan tourism association, although he was unable to afford the trip to receive his award.

Some other Tapalpans also played to the tourist image. They were aware, for example, that truth was less important for weekenders. In a 1998 meeting of the tourism association, one local businessman proposed that they take weekenders around the town square and tell them "the pious lies about the church." The *Guía Verdi*, a guide produced locally for weekenders, included narratives lifted from a book on Mexican legends. My own "History of Tapalpa" sheet

Illustration 12: The late don Chilo, to whom weekenders were referred, in his cantina in Tapalpa (2007).

for tourists told of how Atacco was cursed after two missionaries were killed there. I added that a priest had returned recently to bless the town, which was beginning to prosper again. "You made that up," the Atacco deputy Beto said laughing, and I had to admit that he was right—I had felt that writing for weekenders gave me a license to portray the town in a brighter light.

But that kind of history did not give anyone cultura. Guadalajarans saw Tapalpa not unlike the way Tapalpans saw Atacco: as a rural place in which they might find, at best, rooting in place and what Rulfo called condescendingly "knowledge of the past"—quirky stories, nostalgic memories, and so on. Atacco from the perspective of Tapalpans was ugly and its people were rooted out of stubbornness, while Tapalpa from the perspective of Guadalajarans was pretty and its people were rooted in a quaint, idiosyncratic way. But even so, few Guadalajarans expected Tapalpa to have a full-fledged history or a town historian of the kind that they might find in Guadalajara. Instead, they expected to encounter the folkloric kind of history that don Chilo served up with locally brewed spirits.

How does that compare with Rulfo's take on "this land"? On the one hand, Rulfo emphasizes that "worthy men" had lived in the region, and that it had "yielded fine examples of a living *cultura*." He was presumably referring to the ceramics, pyramids, and ancient tombs found throughout the region that he had discussed in his lecture. On the other hand, Rulfo notes that no one in the present knew who had produced those magnificent ceramics (Rulfo 1986, 70). In a similar vein, he complained of neighboring Michoacán that the Tarascans lacked knowledge of their past, and therefore could not be considered a powerful cultura (48–50). His best hope for the present was, it seems, not cultura, but rooting. Rulfo, too, seemed to see the towns of the region as rural places that were bereft of cultura, rather than places in which cultura was at home.

One group of Guadalajarans did try to juggle both cultura and a measure of rooting. For example, my friend Martha had lived in Tapalpa for a year and owned a country house in an exclusive development outside Tapalpa. Martha complained about the drunken antics of many weekenders, which showed that they lacked cultura—they did not appreciate Tapalpa in the right way. But she also complained about being ignored by the municipal government—this was during the term of Arnoldo Zamora. The country club manager Enrique said, too, that he had encountered resistance from locals, after living in the town for a year. I argue that history offered them a way of claiming some rooting as well as cultura. Martha had conducted research into Tapalpa's history and folklore, including for a postgraduate degree. She sometimes used the locals' ignorance to set her own knowledge in relief. On one trip to an outlying village, Martha and a visiting doctor made much of Rulfo's association with the region (Zárate Hernández 1997, 37–39). She also told us that she had once asked a woman for "pre-Hispanic ruins" in the area and the woman had replied, "telephonic ruins?" That summed up for Martha the lack of interest in their history shown by locals.

Meanwhile, some residents found it difficult to live up to the quaint rooting expected of them. Enrique complained to me that Tapalpan residents spoiled the pueblo típico image of the town with their baseball caps and vulgar music. The four books on Tapalpa presented in the Hilton Hotel, contained only carefully staged photos of residents who fit into the quaint townsfolk role (illustration 13). The *Rough Guide to Mexico* (1994) notes: "Though there's a village feel around the plaza, with its 18th-century wooden portals and two impressive churches, this is actually a fair-sized place, and messy development on the outskirts reflects rapid growth." This "messy development on the outskirts" was due, at least in part, to residents being forced out of the town center by weekenders who had purchased more than half the houses. Weekenders and tourism operators criticized the new houses on the outskirts, especially those that lacked whitewash and tiled roofs. Residents did sometimes turn the tables on their critics, though. For example they criticized the Guadalajaran

Illustration 13: Presentation of books on Tapalpa in the Hilton Hotel, Guadalajara (2005). Note the contrast between the Tapalpan on the screen—taken from one of the books—and the suits on the stage. One of the suits is Rodolfo Fernández, whom I discussed in the previous chapter. The books were published by the Guadalajara newspaper *El Informador*, which was owned by don Carlos, who also owned the hotel shown in illustration 1.

newspaper owner, Carlos Alvarez del Castillo, for using steel girders instead of the traditional oak beams to build a new floor to his hotel (see illustration 1).

While some residents were pushed to the outskirts of Tapalpa, many others left to work in California or in Guadalajara. They felt that this was necessary for economic reasons, but I note in the next section that members of Tapalpa's elite were, like Rulfo, not so sure.

Migrants in California: Neither Rooting nor Cultura

I have said that Tapalpan residents doubted that the "Indians" of Atacco could come up with a full-blown history of their own town, and that Guadalajarans had similar doubts about Tapalpans. But Tapalpan residents, like Rulfo, also doubted that the hundreds of migrants in California could do any better. At the same time, some felt that migrants were losing their rooting—to their hometown and also to the Mexican nation.

People had been leaving Tapalpa for many years to work, to study, and often to live elsewhere, as was shown by a survey that I conducted of two-hundred households in Tapalpa and one-hundred households in Atacco. Mexico's second city, Guadalajara—a fairly prosperous metropolis—was only three hours away even by second-class bus. Some Tapalpans returned every weekend, while others returned less often, especially when their children were born in Guadalajara. For example, my landlady was one of twelve surviving siblings, of whom (unusually) six were still in Tapalpa and six in Guadalajara while two nephews lived in California. Those in Guadalajara kept visiting Tapalpa at weekends and during the holidays, but the ones in California returned less often. Several family members had studied for university degrees in Guadalajara, and were working as professionals there, which was true of many other Tapalpans as well.

I found Tapalpan residents willing to believe that some Tapalpans living in Guadalajara might know Tapalpa's history. In fact, two of the people said to know it had lived much of their lives in Guadalajara. One was the lawyer, Alberto Arámbula, who returned to Tapalpa at weekends to attend to his hotel, and the other was the priest, Father Méndez, who had written on Tapalpa's history. Each had left Tapalpa to study and work in Guadalajara, but returned periodically until their deaths in the 1990s. They had each given talks on Tapalpa's history, and the priest had published on the subject. The municipal chronicler José Fajardo, had worked for years as a teacher in Guadalajara and had published regularly in Guadalajara newspapers.

By contrast, many residents were amused that I went to California in 1998 to ask migrants there for Tapalpa's history. Like Rulfo, some residents accused the migrants in California of lacking not just cultura, but even rooting. Teachers complained that Tapalpan children were just waiting to finish secondary or high school to leave to work in California. I do not know of any Tapalpan who went to California just to study, but they did go to Guadalajara to study. Teachers considered work in construction or kitchens a waste of an education. They were often anti-American, and regretted that their pupils would leave Mexico to work in a nation that was considered materialistic and so bereft of cultura. They noted, too, that migrants lived a life of vice in California, and they were sure that their young pupils would also succumb to this problem. Most migrants in California were young or middle-aged males, although there was an older generation in San Francisco. Employers also often voiced complaints. They grumbled about their workers leaving, and also complained that migrants who returned were reluctant to work for Mexican wages. Employers insisted that there was plenty of work in Tapalpa, and that people left for the north because "they did not how to work." Parents and grandparents were often dependent on the money sent back from California, and did express their appreciation of the "sacrifice" made by their sons and daughters. But they sometimes grumbled, too. One old lady complained of Tapalpan youths that, "all they know is the north" and added, "Before, it was a forgotten north."

During a month of fieldwork in Concord, California in 1998, I found that migrants were surprised that I would go there to ask about Tapalpa's history. I talked to older migrants. They talked patiently—and sometimes passionately—about their memories of Tapalpa, as well as about their experiences in California. But some were puzzled about why I was asking them, rather than the old people still living in the town. One concluded, eventually, that I was asking for his personal "biography" rather than the town's "history." At the same time, I found that the younger migrants in Concord were anxious for knowledge of Tapalpa's history and self-conscious of their ignorance. They wanted me to tell them about Tapalpa's history, which seemed much more interesting and important to them from afar. For example, I was taken on a Saturday night to an apartment nicknamed La Coahuila after the notorious avenue in Tijuana. Several young men sat around drinking beer

Illustration 14: Tapalpans chatting and watching a video of the Tapalpan festival in "La Coahuila" apartment, Concord, California (1998).

and exchanging banter while they watched a video of the religious festival in Tapalpa (illustration 14). "Ask him about your families and your homes," said one of them, "he knows Tapalpa better than any of you." Not only did I know their families, I had never had such an attentive audience for my account of Tapalpa's history. For much of the evening they fired questions at me, while finding it ironic that "those from elsewhere know more than we do."

I asked these migrants about Concord's history, but I found that few were interested or could say much about it. I argue that interest in Concord's history would have suggested rooting in California. Rooting in California was resisted by most Tapalpans—it was reserved for Tapalpa. When I probed them, I found that some had learned something of Concord's history, in spite of themselves. Ramiro, the head of the household where I stayed in Concord, made a point of denying any interest in Concord's history, but turned out to have learned some of its history from his employer. Another said he knew nothing, but then said that Concord was settled first by Indians and later became a hacienda. Migrants often added that California had belonged to Mexico anyway.*

---

* They were, unfortunately, presenting themselves as the very "birds of passage" that critics of immigration have for so long accused them of being—staying only temporarily in the United States while they saved enough money to return to their countries of origin to which they remained loyal (Hansen 2003).

Illustration 15: Corner of the main square of Concord, California (1998). Note the red-tiled roofs, which were in keeping with the "Hispanic" feel of Concord's plaza, a town originally named Todos Santos.

One could, then, deny being rooted or committed to a place, which bears out a critical point of this chapter—belonging is not as simple as it might seem. I have already shown that not everyone had rooting. Federico's group was concerned about people abandoning Atacco, Tapalpan teachers and employers were worried about migration to the United States, and Rulfo was fearful about the region as a whole. I have also presented different notions of rooting. For example, Tapalpans viewed Atacco's residents as stubbornly rooted, while Guadalajarans viewed Tapalpans as quaintly rooted. People could be rooted to several places, although this was not always easy to pull off. Martha had an easy claim to Guadalajara, but she had more trouble combining that with a claim on Tapalpa. I have hinted at a second point: people were rooted to nations as well as to towns. This explains why residents had different expectations of migrants in Guadalajara and in the United States. A third point is that cultura was not any old way of going beyond the immediate. Migrants could travel thousands of miles without laying a claim to cultura, while don Lupe and others could claim cultura while living in their hometowns. But that raises a final question: Did people who had cultura still need rooting?

Cosmopolitan Citizens: Rooting Cultura Back to Place

Rooting was still an issue for individuals who had cultura. Rulfo was himself an example: he had left his hometown for the world of cultura, but was still concerned to show some kind of rooting. Other examples were the Tapalpan lawyer Arámbula, the priest Father Méndez, and the municipal chronicler Fajardo. By showing interest in the history of their hometowns or regions, they could claim rooting while showing off their cultura.

Rulfo's stance toward historical knowledge was similar to Federico's and that of many others in west Mexico. To begin with, Rulfo insisted in his talk on a full-fledged cosmopolitan kind of history, and was keen to show off his credentials. He stressed that historians should work from archives, especially the National Archive in Mexico City, and he also mentioned research done by the National University (Rulfo 1986, 46, 59–60). He had worked for many years in Mexico City as an editor of anthropology texts for the National Indigenist Institute. Rulfo showed, in other words, that he could produce the kind of history that would fly in the world of cultura, even though he qualified his history of Colima as a "hypothesis," explaining that he had not yet conducted enough research (27–28).

At the same time, Rulfo claimed rooting in his lecture by producing the history of the region, although his claim to rooting was a complex one. He identified, at different points of the lecture, with southern Jalisco, west Mexico, and the Mexican nation. Rulfo considered it important that someone should research and write Colima's history, because there was much to write about, and because it would help Colima's inhabitants to appreciate the places where they lived (Rulfo 1986, 48). He regretted that so little history had been written of Colima, although he admitted that Jalisco's history was not much more advanced (59–60). But Rulfo stressed this history of Colima should be produced by people from that region. He made it clear why it was dangerous to leave others to write one's history: much of his lecture was a tirade against historians from the neighboring state of Michoacán, who had claimed that Colima and southern Jalisco were subject to Michoacán in pre-Hispanic times, and that its art was the product of Michoacán's influence (37–38, 48–49). Although Rulfo's lecture was ostensibly about Colima's history, he kept repeating that it really should have been written by the historians from Colima in his audience. He himself seemed more interested in the history of southern Jalisco, where he was born and spent his childhood, and where his family still had some connections—although he did not refer to San Gabriel, the town where he had lived before his father was killed and before his mother died. Rulfo did make some reference to Guadalajara, the city where he spent his teenage years in an orphanage and where much of his extended family continued to live. He was also keen to defend west Mexico as a whole, like many regional intellectuals, against Mexico City historians who played down its archaeology and history (60; Muriá 2003). For example, Rulfo compared ancient Coliman art to that of Central Mexico in its splendor, but he also made it clear that it was not derived from Central Mexican art (Rulfo 1986, 45, 50–51). But he ended by insisting that "*Mexicans* are, as a general rule, a nationalist and rooted people" (65; emphasis added), although clearly he regarded migrants to the United States as exceptions.

Rulfo was far from the only west Mexican with cultura for whom rooting was still an issue. Many individuals with a fair claim to cultura had, like Rulfo, left their hometowns. Like other migrants, they needed to make an effort if they wanted to maintain their rooting. I have described the effort put into producing Tapalpa's history by Arámbula, Méndez, and Fajardo. Fajardo, although born and raised in Tapalpa, had spent many years in Guadalajara, and was largely unknown in Tapalpa when I began fieldwork in 1992, but by 2005 he had become well known for his knowledge of the town's history and was something of a public figure as a result. Some of these individuals were feted by residents of their hometowns and regions, who were delighted to root them back to place. Father Méndez, for example, was listed as a *hijo ilustre* (illustrious son) in the *Monograph of Tapalpa*, penned in 1985 by don Lupe and the library staff; also feted was a poet who had left Tapalpa, but who had written a poem or two about the town (Nava López et al. 1985, 7–11). That allowed residents of the towns to bask in reflected glory, since it made their towns or regions look like cradles for cultura. Federico Munguía, the chronicler of nearby Sayula, describes a nineteenth-century Sayulan lawyer, Joaquín Camberos, as a "man of great *cultura*," who had left to study and practice law in Guadalajara. Munguía adds that Camberos "used to narrate episodes of Universal History in which he was quite knowledgeable." Camberos was offered a government position in Mexico City, but refused because he did not wish to leave his "native land" (Munguía Cárdenas 1976, 149). Camberos's "native land" was in this case the state of Jalisco, but Munguía's description still betrays the mix of cultura and rooting that made for a hijo ilustre. Munguía (1987) also traced the history of Rulfo's family in the region as well as his bibliography. I suspect that Munguía, who is sometimes cited by academics and has had three editions of his local history book published by the state government, may himself end up on the list of hijos ilustres of his town.

By hailing them as hijos ilustres, residents could also make claims on living individuals who, like Rulfo, had made their mark. Muriá (2003, 108) writes of the "brain drain" from Jalisco:

> There have been many émigrés who have not remembered their fellow-countrymen except when receiving some award from them, or when agreeing to take some public post there if the powers-that-be have requested this. But there have been some who have not cut the umbilical cord and who, even when outside their homeland, continue to take an interest in the knowledge and expression of their land.

Rulfo's hosts at the University of Colima were obviously aware of his connections in Guadalajara and in Mexico City, and were keen to claim him as a kind of hijo ilustre. One of the academics in the audience proposed, for example, that Rulfo "be the godfather" of their own efforts to produce Colima's history (Rulfo 1986, 59). In Tapalpa, I heard of people making claims on Arámbula but especially on Luis Enrique Bracamontes, who had been sub-secretary of public works in the federal government from 1958 to 1964. Not everyone agreed that Bracamontes had been faithful to his town and

Illustration 16: Mural in the entrance to Tapalpan municipal library, bearing faces of some hijos ilustres (1999). The man on the right, surrounded by scrolls of paper, is Luis Enrique Bracamontes.

others felt he was too much of a politician, but he was still on the list of hijos ilustres in the *Monograph of Tapalpa*, and the Tapalpan library, founded in 1983, was named after him (Nava López et al. 1985, 7).

Before concluding, I should add that Rulfo did not want his fiction to be read in the way that he wanted his history to be read. In his history lecture, he presented himself as someone who had grown up in the region and who wrote from that perspective (although with due reference to Mexico City archives). By contrast, Rulfo always resisted attempts by literary critics and others to read his fiction in terms of the world in which he spent his childhood. He admitted, at times, that his fiction may have derived from certain experiences or stories he had heard, although at other times he denied this: "Unfortunately I had no one to tell me stories, in our town the people are closed, yes, completely, one is a stranger there" (Rulfo 1992, 383). In any case, Rulfo insisted that his "imagination" had transformed these experiences, and also that his writing owed a heavy debt to foreign writers such as Faulkner and Joyce. He criticized journalists who visited the region in search of Rulfian landscapes and faces. "Haven't you noticed that the people in my fiction do not have faces?" (1998 [1977]). He did not even seem to consider his fiction to be particularly Mexican. Ironically, the editors of his posthumously published lecture added a prologue by the Coliman poet Miguel Romero Solís, who linked Rulfo's history to his fiction. Rulfo was killed by the murmurs, wrote the poet, echoing Rulfo's novel *Pedro Páramo*: "Perhaps, that of which he spoke to us that night, was one of those murmurs, beyond the Revolution, the Reform . . . the waxed dogs and the extraordinary ceramics" (1986, 21–22). But Rulfo himself made no reference to his fiction and no attempt to emulate its astonishing poetics in the lecture on Colima's history.

Rooting, Cultura, and Being a Citizen

If having cultura was linked to being a citizen, so was rooting or being "from here." But cultura and rooting were linked to different aspects of citizenship. I have written of my informants' views, during the interviews about citizenship that I conducted in 2007, about what it took to be a good citizen. Interviewees often talked of citizenship as precisely that—an *ideal of civility* to which all should aspire. Heater (1992) has traced the long tradition of the "civic ideal" of citizenship back to Aristotle, and some republican philosophers continue to extol the virtue of civility (Dagger 1997). But what my interviewees called rooting or being "from here" was about *membership of the town*. That is the aspect of citizenship on which most social scientists have focused, whether writing of the nation (Marshall 2009 [1950]; Turner 2001; Fahrmeir 2007) or of towns and cities (Herzog 2007; Holston and Appadurai 1999).

If cultura was hard to pull off, rooting was not straightforward either. Membership in a community was complicated by people moving from place to place, including to California. Moreover, not everyone gave the same value to rooting. A middle-aged Tapalpan woman, very active in community groups, said that she could hardly imagine living outside Tapalpa. Other informants felt more footloose—they had lived outside the town for extended periods, and could imagine doing so again. Some said that "community" was something that served to exclude them. Two businessmen from Guadalajara, for example, complained of local elites intent on excluding people "not from here" from the spoils of Tapalpa's tourism. Finally, attempting to combine cultura and rooting could be difficult as well. Having cultura involved tapping into wider networks of learning and civility, which could jeopardize rooting in place, perhaps even for such dignitaries as Rulfo and Appiah.

The question of citizenship of towns and cities begs the question of how that citizenship relates to national citizenship. Part III asks whether good citizens of towns, such as don Lupe, were also considered good citizens of the Mexican nation. My focus, of course, is on Mexico's history: what that history meant to people and how they linked it to Tapalpa's history.

PART III

OTHER HISTORIES

National History and the History of Virgins

CHAPTER SIX

Towns and Nations

Different Histories, Different Citizenships

I found that, just as Rulfo said, Mexicans liked to talk Mexican history more than natives of many other countries did theirs. Mexican history came up in many conversations around Tapalpa, Zamora, and Concord. I even witnessed a debate between two Mexicans in an Aberdeen bar, just before a World Cup game, about whether the Aztecs or the Zapotecs had taken over Oaxaca and built Monte Albán. "Are you really talking about history?" asked a Venezuelan, incredulously.

Despite their interest in Mexican history, few Tapalpans connected what they knew of the town's history with what they knew of Mexican history. My main explanation for this is not that Tapalpans resisted Mexican history because they disagreed with it, although that is possible and scholars have written of Mexicans resisting and reinterpreting official history (Stephen and Pisa 1998; Nugent and Alonso 1994). Instead, I argue that Mexico's history was so different in content and form to Tapalpa's history that it was hard to connect them. One result was that few people could challenge Mexico's history by playing Tapalpa's history off against it—that is, by using what they knew of Tapalpa's history to challenge what they had been taught of Mexican history. What had happened in Mexican history was left to national historians, who were in a different league. Even regional historians, such as Juan Rulfo and José María Muriá, struggled to have much impact on national history.

Something similar was true of citizenship. Scholars have identified as "urban citizenship" a range of identities and activities of recent years, including struggles to assert "rights to the city" such as access to public space or utilities (Holston and Appadurai 1999; Sassen 2002; Isin 2007). I observe in this chapter that the relationship between urban and national citizenship, like that of urban and national history, is a complex one (Gordon and Stack 2007). Tapalpans considered themselves citizens of their town as well as citizens of Mexico, but the citizenship of towns and nations were different in kind and there was not much connection between them.

Talking Mexican History

Although I was interested in Tapalpa's history in 1992, I heard a fair amount of Mexico's history around Tapalpa. I was told of events such as the Spanish Conquest, the wars of independence, and the Mexican Revolution, as well as of characters such as Pancho Villa, Emiliano Zapata, Miguel Hidalgo, and Hernán Cortés. But what I heard sounded different from Tapalpa's history. It was not just that people said different things, but that Tapalpa's history and Mexico's history were two different ways of talking and of writing. Tapalpans talking about Tapalpa's history focused almost exclusively on what in fact happened, or on who might know what in fact happened. When talking about Mexico's history, by contrast, they argued about almost everything but what in fact happened. I often heard Tapalpans boast about how much history Mexico had, and especially that Mexico had far more history than the United States. I also heard people talk about Mexico's history, but they argued less about what happened than about who knew which episodes of Mexican history (and some said that foreigners knew more Mexican history than they did). Several were skeptical about what they heard of Mexican history. I heard several people complain about the new textbooks introduced in 1992, just as newspapers listed the errors contained in the new books. Others made fun of what was taught as official history, usually to make a political point. A left-wing Tapalpan high school teacher put on a play in the town square of Tapalpa in 1998 that parodied the official version of Mexican history. People argued, too, about what should be taught at school and how. Another teacher complained that Mexico's pre-Hispanic past was cut from the national curriculum in the textbooks introduced in 2004. Finally, people drew lessons from Mexican history but also argued about those lessons. Not all agreed, for example, that the neo-Zapatistas in Chiapas were right to claim Zapata as their inspiration. National history was, moreover, not just the subject of talk and writing like Tapalpa's history. It lived in places such as the Aztec and Mayan pyramids, in museums and in cities, and was played out or commemorated in all kinds of ceremonies. The best-known ceremony was the *Grito* (Cry of Independence), offered by the municipal president at midnight on September 15, from the balcony of the town hall, commemorating the call to arms of Miguel Hidalgo in 1810. Mexican history also featured in a series of parades throughout the year. One was the parade

Illustration 17: Independence Day parade in Tapalpa (1999).

Illustration 18: Revolution Day parade in Tapalpa (1999).

of the Mexican Revolution on November 20. Teachers marshaled their pupils to parade in school uniforms on September 16, and in sports uniforms on November 20 (illustrations 17 and 18).

Tapalpans did sometimes try to connect Mexico's history to Tapalpa's history. In their *Monograph of Tapalpa*, the library staff with the help of don Lupe placed Tapalpa's history quite confidently within regional history and, to some extent, within Mexican history. Federico's group had, as I have said, alluded to Tarascan pyramids in their talk of ancient remains around Atacco. A storekeeper, don Elías, said that Pedro Zamora, who burned half of Tapalpa in 1917, was in league with the famous revolutionary Pancho Villa. And so on. People did something similar in other towns that I visited. In the nearby Sierra del Tigre, a town librarian deftly intertwined stories of the Cristeros with an account of the Mexican Revolution (as I tried to do in my introduction). Why did people attempt to connect their towns' history with Mexican history? One reason was to argue for their town's importance in the region or nation. Fajardo did that in his articles in *El Informador*, as did don Lupe and the library staff in their *Monograph of Tapalpa*, especially by boasting of Tapalpa's hijos ilustres. Sometimes they were keen to give their towns a very particular place in the nation. Florencia Mallon observes, for example, that town chroniclers in the Sierra de Puebla were careful to place their towns on either the liberal or conservative side in nineteenth-century Mexican history (Mallon 1995, 242–44). Even those who were critical of Mexican history were still happy to make the link. The author of a local history of San Sebastián del Oeste, a town above Puerto Vallarta, railed against the Mexican Revolution, which had brought only suffering to the town, and objected strenuously to the schoolteacher's decision in naming the town square after the Mexican Revolution. Rulfo, meanwhile, complained bitterly in his lecture at the Universidad de Colima about "centralist" history, as did Muriá in his writing and in my interview with him (Muriá 2003; Rulfo 1986, 48).

At first it seemed to me that Tapalpans were substituting official history for the history that they told of Tapalpa. I felt that I had found an alternative version of national history that challenged the official version, as other scholars have described (e.g., Stephen 1997; Nugent and Alonso 1994). My original project in Tapalpa, as I explained in part I, was to write a history of the Cristero rebellion. Most studies that I had read described the Cristero rebellion as a reaction to the Mexican Revolution of 1910 to 1917, as had the librarian in the Sierra del Tigre. In 1992, I visited the Museum of the Mexican

Revolution in the neighboring state of Michoacán. The museum director, Luís Prieto Reyes, talked about the Mexican Revolution as he showed me around. When I observed that Tapalpans gave a quite different history of the period, the director made a curious comment: "Tapalpa must be a pretty town." I replied that it was a pretty town. He explained, "In my experience, all reactionary towns are pretty." Certainly, I found that many Tapalpans complained of much of what the Mexican government—and the museum director—was quick to boast (Benjamin 2000). Landowners in the Sierra complained about the land reform and I have said that Andrés in Atacco was critical of the ejidatarios' dependence on the government that had given them land, as well as refusing to name Atacco's streets after the usual Mexican revolutionaries. Don Lupe, while he was municipal president for the third time in the 1980s, had named a new Tapalpan street in Tapalpa after the last hacienda owner, Vidal Vizcaíno. Several elderly people, although by no means all, did speak well of the Cristero rebels, and scholars have identified the Cristero rebellion as a symptom of the region's reaction to the revolutionary regime (Butler 2005).

What surprised me, however, was that Tapalpans only rarely made the connection. They did not often link the Cristeros that they had heard about and the Mexican Revolution that they celebrated on November 20, and neither did they play off Tapalpa's history against Mexico's history. On the one hand, Luis González y González (1968) did pitch his microhistory of San José de Gracia—which inspired my own attempt at Tapalpa's history—as a challenge to Mexico's history. He wrote, for example, that news of the Mexican Revolution had less impact in the town than the ashes that fell that year from a nearby volcano. And he argued that San José had suffered the Revolution without reaping its benefits. González y González did not question the idea that there was a Mexican Revolution—that the multiple conflicts of those years added up to a single national revolution—but he did use microhistory to query what was usually recounted of that Revolution, including the extent to which it was a genuinely national movement. Tapalpans, on the other hand, argued about the lessons to be learned from Mexican history, such as whether politicians had betrayed the Mexican Revolution just as Zapata was betrayed, and they were sometimes skeptical of what they had been taught in the classroom. But they did not use Tapalpa's history as an antidote to Mexican history in the way that González y González did. Only rarely did they make Pedro Zamora into the "dark side" of the Mexican Revolution or even into a revolutionary, or the Cristero soldiers into champions of the people against the revolutionaries. Similarly, the author of San Sebastián del Oeste's history complained that the town had received only injury from the Mexican Revolution and none of the gains, but that is still an argument about how to interpret the events of the Revolution, not an attempt to produce an alternative history of it.

One explanation is that Tapalpans, although hostile to the official history of the Mexican Revolution, preferred to avoid challenging the official history explicitly and instead simply told a different history of what had happened in the Sierra. It is no doubt true that in a one-party state—the Partido Revolucionario Institucional (PRI, Institutional Revolutionary Party) ruled Mexico from 1929 up to 2000—an explicit challenge to official history is unwise. By 1998, when the schoolteacher parodied official history in the play performed in town square, the PRI had lost much of its power, even before losing the presidential election in 2000. Perhaps Tapalpans were being diplomatic in not pointing out that what they knew of Tapalpa's history flew in the face of what they were taught as Mexico's history.

However, I believe that the main reason that Tapalpans only rarely linked Tapalpa's history with Mexican history was not because they disagreed with Mexican history but because they were different kinds of knowledge. What people learned of the two histories—and how they learned it—was very different. Some, like Fajardo and don Elías, were better able to bridge this gap, to splice together stories, even if sometimes in awkward ways. But most had considerable difficulty. Indeed, most Tapalpans found it hard to situate the Mexican Revolution at all. On several occasions, I interrupted a conversation about Tapalpa's revolutions with the question: "What about the Mexican Revolution?" People replied in various ways, but the response was typically hesitant and stumbling. Some people mentioned a date, usually either 1810 or 1910; or a name or two—Pancho Villa, Emiliano Zapata, Miguel Hidalgo; or an incident, such as the betrayal of Emiliano Zapata. But most, if they could, then sought the quickest way back to Tapalpa's history. Not because they had nothing to say about Mexico's history or because they were hostile to it, but simply because they found the link difficult to make.

Making the connection was hard because they had learned Mexico's history in a different way from Tapalpa's history. They had heard, on the one hand, about a series of revolutions that had occurred during the youth of the town's elderly people. They had learned, on the other hand, that the Mexican Revolution was not one in a series of revolutions, but a singular Revolution. Many found it difficult to relate this singular event to the series of Tapalpa's revolutions. Moreover, people usually dated Tapalpa's revolutions by reference to other events such as births, marriages, and deaths, while they located the Mexican Revolution by dates learned for school exams or displayed on banners in parades. In fact, many associated the Mexican Revolution less with the years of chronology and more with the days of the calendar, particularly November 20, the annual commemoration of the Mexican Revolution. As a result, they found it easier to link it to other calendar dates, such as September 16, Mexican Independence Day, than to Tapalpa's revolutions. Small wonder that Tapalpans listed revolutionaries like Pancho Villa and Emiliano Zapata together with Miguel Hidalgo, better known by historians as the father of Mexican independence.

Leaving National History for National Historians

One effect of the gap between what people learned of Tapalpa's history and of Mexico's history was that Tapalpa's history was little influenced by schooling. Schooling did have some effect on what was told of Tapalpa's history. It made the idea of history widely familiar and gave a sense of value to it. Schooling also gave people a reason to ask questions about Tapalpa's history:

Illustration 19: Float in Independence Day parade in Tapalpa (1999). The boy raising his hand represents Miguel Hidalgo giving a speech, presumably to the peasants in the foreground.

their children or grandchildren might be asked to write a project on it. I will concede in part IV that some things found their way from official history into Tapalpa's history, especially the idea of *mestizaje* (literally, racial mixing). On the whole, though, what Tapalpans learned at school of Mexican history was insulated from what they learned outside the classroom, notwithstanding the introduction of regional history as a school subject from the 1980s (e.g., Becerra et al. 1997; Muriá 1995).

Another effect was that few if anyone around Tapalpa produced knowledge about what in fact happened in Mexican history. I heard arguments about who did what in Tapalpa's revolutions but not usually about who did what in Mexico's Revolution; there was not much that they could add to it. Not everyone had the same authority to talk about Tapalpa's revolutions, but everyone at least knew someone who did. By contrast, they had learned about the Mexican Revolution in school classrooms and in civic parades, places in which there was little or no ability to question it. Schoolchildren dutifully learned the events, places, and protagonists of the cosmic struggle that was Mexico's history. Many came to feel some pride in the pre-Conquest history and that of Independence; some groups such as the ejidatarios in Atacco said on occasion that they owed their lands to the Mexican Revolution. Others were skeptical, we have seen. Some took a stand, for example, on what they believed were the true lessons of Mexican history, while others doubted what they had been taught at school or celebrated in parades. But it was very much the skepticism of the backseat driver—without the authority to back it up. Few tried to offer an authoritative alternative to that history, much less one based on Tapalpa's history. Most people left the knowledge of Tapalpa's history to the likes of don Lupe or José Fajardo; by contrast, even history schoolteachers saw their role as simply to impart knowledge of Mexico's history, not to produce that knowledge themselves. If the history of towns was skewed, in other words, the history of nations was even more skewed.

Instead, Mexico's history was left to national historians, who were in a league of their own. There were many disputes among these historians. The museum director whom I interviewed criticized the work of Luis González y González, as well as Jean Meyer's history of the Cristero rebellion, which he saw as reactionary. There were even differences between what made it into the textbooks and what was acted out in national pageantry. In 1995, for example, the government of President Zedillo introduced a new set of textbooks from which the Niños Héroes (Child Heroes) had been neatly excised. The Niños Héroes were a group of children who, according to the old textbooks, had thrown themselves off the walls of Chapultepec Castle, in the center of Mexico City, rather than submitting to the American invaders in 1846. The Education Ministry decided to jettison the Niños Héroes from the textbooks since there was no historical record of their existence. Notwithstanding, President Zedillo went on to commemorate Child Heroes Day later that year. Fajardo, don Lupe, and Munguía were, in any case, excluded from this kind of dispute about what happened in Mexico's history. Luis González y González was unusual in arguing that historians should pay attention to the writings of town chroniclers, but he went on to observe that those chroniclers lacked the "global vision" necessary to write national history (González y González 1986, 12). Even regional historians like Muriá, who themselves looked down on local chroniclers even while sponsoring them, were given short shrift on the national stage.

I have said that historians of towns got cultura from their knowledge, and that it made them eminent citizens of their towns. What did national historians get from their knowledge of history? One obvious answer is that it gave them, as professionals, a salary. Claudio Lomnitz (2001, 213–27) has noted that academic salaries were eroded by the 1980s crisis, and that some historians turned to a more commercially appealing kind of history. His prime example is the historian Enrique Krauze, author of a best-selling series on Mexican presidents and a regular on television chat shows. But national history also made for eminent citizens of Mexico. There was a long tradition of intellectuals holding government positions but many other intellectuals who did not take government positions still had a voice in Mexican politics. The novelists Elena Poniatowksa and Carlos Fuentes, along with Octavio Paz and the essayist Carlos Monsivais, are obvious examples. Among historians, perhaps the most striking twentieth-century example was Daniel Cosío Villegas, one of the few *críticos permitidos* (permitted critics) at a time when critics often found themselves in trouble. A more recent example is Héctor Aguilar Camín, a historian (and novelist) who has emerged as a distinguished commentator on Mexican politics. The same was true, on a lesser scale, of some regional historians; I have mentioned that Muriá was elected councilor of the Zapopan district of Guadalajara. National historians could address national issues either through newspaper columns or speeches or, more subtly, through the history that they produced. Roger Bartra argued in 1989 that Luis González y González spoke for a "rustic fringe" of small holding cattle ranchers and agriculturalists—bastions of Mexico's "new conservatism"—who were supposed to have suffered the Revolution without benefiting from it (González y González 1986, 66–69). Muriá, meanwhile, used the history of Jalisco to champion states' rights, especially those of his adoptive state, Jalisco. Muriá relished the fact that centralists had objected to parts of his history of Jalisco textbook (1995). For example, he said they had complained about the section of his text in which he said little news of independence had reached Guadalajara, an obvious echo of González y González's claim about news of the Mexican Revolution in San José de Gracia.

Citizens of Towns, Citizens of Nations

I explained in part II there were several ways in which knowing history was linked to being citizens. I said that knowing history was a sign of cultura, which was linked in turn to being a good citizen; I showed that some people were better at knowing history than others, which made them more eminent citizens, and ended by saying that history could also be a sign of rooting, which was also important for citizenship, and that cultura and rooting were sometimes difficult to combine. I focused in those chapters on the history told of towns and cities, insisting that history was not only about nations. Similarly, I suggested that people did not just link citizenship to the Mexican nation but also to towns and cities. People did not usually call themselves citizens of Tapalpa, but when I asked my interviewees in 2007 whether they were citizens of Tapalpa as well as of Mexico, most replied that they were.

However, the citizenship of towns and cities was different in kind to Mexican citizenship, just as the history of towns and Mexico's history. I have focused in this chapter on the relation between the history that people told of nations and what they told of towns, claiming that people had trouble connecting the two because they were different in kind. As national citizens, Tapalpans argued about national politics and what it meant to be Mexican, grumbling and doubting, while going through the paces in the school classrooms and in civic parades. Some did seek out connections with key players in the national arena. Don Lupe was not just an individual with cultura, for example, but someone who was well connected with politicians in Guadalajara and even Mexico City. Don Lupe and other Tapalpans also celebrated Luis Enrique Bracamontes, who as national subsecretary of public works had ordered the building of the road up to Tapalpa. Both the library and a main street were named after Bracamontes, while the primary school was named after his wife. On the whole, though, I found that people experienced being citizens of Tapalpa rather differently from being Mexican citizens. For one thing, at least some Tapalpans could aspire to being part of a public arena in the town, where their views might just count for something. Or, as one young Tapalpan put it, "here in Tapalpa I am someone's son whereas in Guadalajara I am just an *hijo de la chingada*" (son of a bitch).

I have found a similar gap in my fieldwork in 2007. Interviewees were happy to describe themselves as Mexican citizens, but some distinguished between their relationship with their town or city and with the nation. The following example is from an interview in 2007 with a small businessman named Roberto in the city of Zamora, Michoacán:

Trevor: Do you feel like a citizen of Zamora or just a Mexican citizen?

Roberto: I could sometimes feel like a citizen and sometimes more of Zamora, because this is where I am.

Trevor: And is it the same thing or is there much difference between one [kind of] citizenship and the other?

Roberto: It's clear to me that your real residence is where you are; the rest is like a part of the organization that you need. I think that only a few people are permanently moving and traveling. I have the idea that Mexican-ness is sometimes artificial. Because what we learn of history is very much falsified—no one tells you for example that all our national heroes were priests and had wives and children, which was perhaps common. They tell you of dates that we celebrate as if they were a big deal and here in Zamora there's a house in which Hidalgo spent a night and, well, it has a plaque and I don't know what. And sometimes they are wars and battles that meant nothing to Zamora. It's as if you were governed by the king of Castile or of Aragón, it makes no difference. It would be the same if he were from Mexico City and governed you well. It will affect you whether he's good or bad, but that's it. In that sense I am more rooted as a Zamoran than as a Mexican. Even though the origin of the two kinds of information is different. At school I never saw anything of Zamoran history, what I know is firstly because of my family and because I was interested in knowing it. In my family they were never complicit with the school in telling me that everything I was taught was right. My father was very critical about history. The [political] cartoonist Rius was a cousin of my father. During a time when he was being attacked my father hid him. My father was fairly rebellious; he didn't accept easily what the government imposed, including what was taught at school about the meaning of being Mexican.

Note that Roberto identifies closely with his city, Zamora, and when asked, considers himself more a citizen of Zamora than of Mexico. Another interviewee concluded that being Mexican was more of an identity that people shared, rather than something they did together. When I asked what Mexicans did in common, one or two said voting but several others said religion—a few mentioned the cult of the Virgin of Guadalupe. Some also referred to the "patriotic symbols" used in the public festivals in which schoolchildren participate and others observe. Even though I had not discussed my work on history with Roberto, he followed up that contrast between Zamoran and Mexican citizenship by contrasting the Mexican history he had learned at school with Zamora's history. He does so precisely by stressing the "origin of the information [of each]." Roberto knew Zamora's history, he tells us, because of his family and because he was interested in knowing it. Again, though, he does not offer an alternative

Illustration 20: Procession in honor of the Virgin de Guadalupe in Tapalpa's patron festival (1999). Note that the children are dressed in "typical" Mexican folk costumes.

history—a different account of what in fact happened—but instead is mainly being skeptical of what he had learned at school and what to make of it.

Towns, Nations, and the Virgin

I return in part IV to the relation between national and urban citizenship. It is often argued that the urban citizenship and history of early modern Europe were both supplanted by the national citizenship and history of the modern era, but I will suggest that urban citizenship and history have never quite gone away. I also discuss another kind of history that I encountered: I heard people tell and write history not just of towns and nations but also of Catholic icons, including the Virgin of Guadalupe. But I focus on the histories of the Virgin of Defense, who was worshipped throughout the Sierra.

CHAPTER SEVEN

Histories of the Virgin

The Higher Ground of Secular History

History was not just told of towns and nations. I also heard and read histories of Catholic figures, especially the Virgen de la Defensa (Virgin of Defense), who spent most of the year in a town near Tapalpa. Before going to Mexico, I had often heard it said that history was a secular kind of knowledge. I took this to mean that God was left out of history altogether, so it would make no difference whether one believed in God or not. But I found in Mexico that God and other figures of devotion, such as the Virgin of Defense, did crop up in things that were told as history. I felt initially that such histories were not secular but religious before realizing—after reading anthropologists such as Talal Asad (2003), Timothy Fitzgerald (2007), and Michael Lambek (2003)—that the relationship between "secular" and "religious" was more complex than it seemed. Some of the Virgin's histories were still secular, I decided, but in a broader sense of the term. Even if they did not banish divine agency altogether, they still placed divine agency outside the main body of the narrative (Stack 2007[a]).

As I have done for the history of towns and nations, I ask what people got from the history of the Virgin of Defense and especially what authority they gained. Knowing the Virgin's history was less obviously linked to citizenship than knowing Tapalpan or Mexican history. But both history and citizenship did share a secular perspective. Doing history and being citizens involved setting aside religious beliefs and, if only for a moment, bracketing divine agency. Perhaps for that reason, the eminent citizens don Lupe and Fajardo are among my examples of those giving secular histories of the Virgin. However, I will note that even priests and lay Catholic leaders sometimes provided secular histories of the Virgin, and I will suggest that the authority they gained helped to make up for the authority they had lost in other spheres—not least since priests lost their political rights after the Mexican Revolution.

Intimate Encounters and Mystical Monologues

Devotional practices, predominantly Catholic, permeated the lives of most Tapalpan residents. People crossed themselves publicly, they wore badges of their faith including emblems of saints and virgins, and they talked about the objects of their devotion. Many of these practices were closely identified with the town as a whole. The parish church was visible from any point in the surrounding countryside and towered over the public plaza. I was also woken constantly during religious festivities by the sound of rockets being fired at dawn and the passing of brass bands through the streets. Priests enjoyed considerable authority in Tapalpa, and I often heard people refer to what priests said, whether in a sermon, a meeting, or a social gathering.

Many Tapalpans professed devotion to the Virgin of Defense. The Virgin spent most of the year in a nearby town of Juanacatlán, and also stayed in another town, Atemajac. But she visited Tapalpa for two months each year, and her only rival in the devotion of many Tapalpans was the town's patron, the Virgin of Guadalupe. To describe the Virgin of Defense as an object of devotion is perhaps misleading, since she was anything but a passive object for her faithful. Many Tapalpans enjoyed an intimate relationship with the Virgin, expressed in terms of trust, seduction, and gift exchange. Tapalpans prayed to her for miracles and made her promises of all kinds, such as to walk with her from Juanacatlán to Tapalpa each year. There was much give and take between what Tapalpans did for her and what she did for them. Both depended, my landlady Teresa said, on "the faith you have in her."

I heard many narratives of intimate encounters between the Virgin and her faithful. For example, when I asked Toni, a twenty-year-old Tapalpan, for the Virgin's history, he wondered whether I meant the history of her healing, adding that the Virgin had healed many people through miracles. I explained that I meant instead how the Virgin came to the Sierra. He recalled that the catechists in Juanacatlán spoke of the Virgin's history and of a booklet that they had written. Toni could not remember exactly what they had said, but he knew it had something to do with a plague and also oppression. The catechists had promised to send Toni the booklet but they never did. Note that Toni's first response was to assume that I meant the Virgin's miracles. I have mentioned that people sometimes talked of miracles, which ranged from healing to passing exams. A Tapalpan lady, Francisca, explained that miracles were dependent on faith. She told me that she had once prayed to the Virgin of Defense when she was leaving Tapalpa for Juanacatlán, asking her to intercede before God to reunite her son with his wife. That same week, Francisca said, the couple got back together. The Virgin is a miracle-working protagonist of these narratives, as much as the faithful who seek and

Illustration 21: Poster of the Virgin of Defense's annual visit to Tapalpa (2004). Obviously the poster is focused on the parish church and it does not show the whole town, but it still gives an indication of the church's imposing size.

Illustration 22: The Virgin of Defense in procession from Juanacatlán to Tapalpa for her annual visit (2005). Note the video camera.

welcome her intervention. Moreover, both Toni and Francisca clearly identify with the faithful, and offer their narrative as testimony to the Virgin's grace.

Accounts of the Virgin's origins were also often intimate. I was sent to talk to a ninety-five-year-old lady, Josefina, in the third town visited by the Virgin, Atemajac:

> The poor suffered a lot here. Two persons from here [Atemajac] and two from Juanacatlán decided to go to visit a bishop—I don't remember his name. He took this image, and said: "This is going to be your Defense." Then the four of them brought the Sacred Virgin back here. The two from Juanacatlán decided to take it to Juanacatlán. That is the history of the Virgin. But guess what? Four years ago, the Sacred Virgin must have wanted to stay here—she didn't fit in any of the glass cases [in which she is carried]. The priest shed tears, saying that "we only brought you on a visit." Then she allowed herself to enter into her case. We have an immense faith. She's going to arrive here [at a chapel close to Josefina's home] on the 6th, and then she'll go to the parish church. What do you think about that? Many people come on Sundays to visit her. There used

to be many drunks and mariachi music. Now there's none of that, just religion. Having seen the Sacred Virgin, he [the parish priest] said to them, "Do you want the Virgin or alcohol?"

The first part of Josefina's narrative, on the Virgin's origin, might seem secular because the Virgin does not act in her own right. Rather than finding her own way to Juanacatlán, for example, the bishop gives the Virgin to the four locals, who bring her back to Juanacatlán. I argue, however, that Josefina is making the Virgin wait in the wings. Note how easily Josefina moves from the Virgin's origins to her miraculous reluctance to leave Juanacatlán. Josefina tells the origins of the Virgin as a prelude to her present-day miracles.

Josefina, like many elderly residents of the Sierra, gave the parish priest a prominent role in her narrative. Some written histories also gave pride of place to the role of the clergy, and stressed their privileged relationship to the Virgin. One example was a chapter on the Virgin that appeared in a book published in 1954, entitled *Marian Iconography of the Archdiocese of Guadalajara* (Orozco 1954, 209–18). The author was Father Luis Enrique Orozco, a priest of the archdiocese. The history was published by a Catholic press and was intended, no doubt, for the priesthood within and beyond the archdiocese and for other learned Catholics of the archdiocese. Father Orozco focuses much of his chapter on the Indians' journey to the city of Puebla, on the generosity of the Bishop there who gave them the Virgin, and on the priests who later sponsored the building of the church (212–16). However, Father Orozco brings the Virgin out of the wings when he can cite documentary testimony of her acts. He narrates, for example, the "favors" granted by the Virgin to her first owner, the seventeenth-century hermit, Juan Bautista, before she was acquired by the Bishop of Puebla (212–13). Father Orozco also describes the "coronation" of the Virgin in 1920 by the Archbishop of Guadalajara as a "favor" granted to the Archbishop by the Virgin (215–16). At several points Father Orozco uses "miraculous" as an epithet for the Virgin. Father Orozco, writing before the Second Vatican Council plays up the role of the clergy. He gives pride of place to the bishop who gave the image to the Indians, and to the priests who encouraged her cult. For example, he includes the names and titles of all the clergy present at the Virgin's coronation in 1920 (215–16). Father Orozco stresses throughout the clergy's struggle to guide and correct the wayward Indians of the Sierra. In another section, Father Orozco notes approvingly that one parish priest had banned an Indian festival for "irreverence to the Virgin" (214–15). He also writes that the people of Juanacatlán had accused another parish priest of making a copy of the Virgin so he could keep the original for himself. Their accusation only proved, he concludes, the qualities "so unique to the indigenous race . . . lazy, materialistic, and stubborn" (216).

Secular Histories

Together with narratives of intimate encounters and mystical monologues, I found several histories of the Virgin of Defense that took what I am calling a secular perspective. The anthropologist Michael Lambek (2003, 3) defines it beautifully as a perspective by which one looks in "from a position that is ostensibly outside it" on the religious devotion of others (or even one's own). Another metaphor for the secular is offered by Michel de Certeau (1993), in his study of the early modern rise of secular history:

> [Contemporary] historians spontaneously take their task to be the need to determine what a field delineated as "religious" can teach them about a society. . . . The very [social] questions that [early modern historians] had to explain through a truth (God, Providence, etc.) have become what makes their explanations intelligible to us. Between their time and ours, the signifier and the signified have castled. (Certeau 1988, 138)

Religion and the secular have "castled" in the sense that early modern historians looked in on society from the ground of religion; contemporary historians look in on religion from the ground of the secular. Histories are secular when narrators bracket divine agency—whether of God or saints and virgins—and tell of the devotion of their human protagonists as if from outside. Secular history is told from an outside that encompasses religion and from which narrators can look in on religion. Academic historians have not been the only ones to take such a secular perspective—a wide range of people did in the Sierra.

Some secular histories were produced within a secularist context, such as in government documents. One example was the *Monograph of Tapalpa* (Nava López et al. 1985). I have said that the *Monograph* was often consulted by visitors to Tapalpa's library, including schoolchildren who had been sent to produce projects of local history, and bureaucrats who needed a section on Tapalpa's history for municipal reports. The *Monograph* began with three one-page sections on "Historical Data," "Civic Status," and "Spiritual Conquest." These were followed by a section entitled "Our Lady of Defense of Tapalpa." Why was a section on the Virgin included in a document produced and kept within the secularist context of a municipal library? The librarian explained in a 2004 interview that the authors were all devotees of the Virgin, and that they considered the Virgin important to the town and the Sierra (Nava López et al. 1985, 5). She had not thought twice about this, although she did see the objection when I raised it. I argue that they also had another reason for including the section on the Virgin. The authors had lifted the first four sections of the *Monograph*, almost word for word, from Father Orozco's chapter (1985, 2, 4–5; Orozco 1954, 209–18). Father Orozco's chapter was one of the only written sources available at that time, and his whole chapter led up to the section on the Virgin of Defense, which would therefore have been difficult to cut. The *Monograph* authors had, in any case, secularized Father Orozco's narrative. They cut the sections that referred to the "favors" performed by the Virgin, and they also cut the section in which Father Orozco censured the Indians for "irreverence" to the Virgin. The authors kept their distance from the "Indians" who, together with the clergy, were the protagonists of the history. I have said that very few people in the Sierra considered themselves to be Indians in the 1990s. They did not attempt to bring the history up to the present day—to claim that Tapalpa was still a Catholic town, for example. The "Our" in the section title might hint at their devotion, but this was the Virgin's official title and it was also the title of Father Orozco's chapter. Moreover, the authors turned Orozco's chapter in a book on Catholic icons into a mere section in an overwhelmingly secular monograph. There is some allusion to Catholic faith in other sections. The preceding section focuses on the "Spiritual Conquest," the only event listed under "Festivities" is the Virgin of Guadalupe's festival, and a poem by a Tapalpan poet is included. But the *Monograph* as a whole presents a township that was legally founded and that has progressed since then, although without losing its traditions. The Virgin is encompassed within that secular context—she is just one aspect or episode of the township's history and tradition (Nava López et al. 1985).

Other secular histories were produced by narrators who did not share the devotion of their protagonists. I was the only one to write this kind of history but others accepted the validity of such a history. The history that I wrote was not of the Virgin of Defense, but of a Tapalpan church dedicated to another virgin, the Virgin of Mercedes. I published this history to raise funds for the restoration of that church. The Virgin does not act in her own right in my narrative and neither does God. I did not rule out the involvement of God and the Virgin, but I still chose to bracket their agency in my narrative. What I gave was a narrative, sufficient in itself, of the human work that went into building that church (Stack 1994). For example, I argued that the person who sponsored the building of the church did so because of his devotion to the Virgin of Mercedes, rather than arguing that the Virgin had moved him to build the church. A prologue and an epilogue were added to my text by Luz María Escoto, the wife of one of the members of the restoration committee. I read a draft of the prologue and asked for the religious referents to be removed. When the printed copies appeared, however, her prologue was again full of saints and martyrs devoted to the Virgin, and Escoto had added an epilogue that was a prayer to the Virgin. I felt that she had compromised my text with her prologue and epilogue. Escoto's prologue implied that I was also motivated by love for the Virgin, while her epilogue turned my history into an act of devotion rather than of fund raising. Later I decided that I had overestimated the difference between Escoto's perspective and mine. I began with a narrow conception of the secular, one that excluded any mention of divine agency; in this reading, she clearly subverted the secular tone of my text. Significantly, however, Escoto made few if any changes to the main body of my text. Why did she not do so? One reason was that she felt that a piece of secular narration made for a perfectly good act of devotion to the Virgin. That fits the broader model of secular narration that I have proposed. Divine agency (and thus one's own devotion) is bracketed within the main body of the narrative, but there are plenty of other places to put devotion—in this case, the prologue and epilogue. Meanwhile, others accepted the possibility of a secular history of the Virgin, even if they did not take this perspective themselves. Indeed, they accepted that someone like me could narrate the Virgin's history even without sharing their devotion. The church restoration committee, for example, was aware that I was not one of the faithful, but they still accepted my offer to write a history of the church. On many other occasions, people referred to my history of the Virgin without worrying about my own devotion or lack thereof. People raised quibbles about the historical detail of my narrative but, as far as I know, not about my suitability as an author.

Some of these secular histories were produced under the auspices of the Church, including histories that stressed the human struggle for social justice rather than the Virgin's miraculous favors. One was published in 2002

Illustration 23: Presentation of Martín González's history in the ex-parish church, now the municipal cultural forum (2005). At the table from left to right are the municipal chronicler, José Fajardo, the parish priest, Martín González, a chronicler from a nearby town, and an unknown person. The speaker is a priest born in Tapalpa but with a parish in Ciudad Guzmán.

by Martín González, who lived in Ciudad Guzmán, the regional capital of southern Jalisco and seat of the diocese (illustration 23). González was as closely connected to the church as Escoto—in fact, his history was published by the Atemajac parish—although his brand of Catholicism was different from hers. González had rewritten the Virgin's history in the spirit of liberation theology—hence his focus on the "peripheral and the marginalized." The Bishop of Ciudad Guzmán had promoted liberation theology since the founding of the diocese in 1972, and González explained in an interview that he intended his history to help revive that movement in the diocese. Like my own history of the Tapalpan church, there are no miracles in his narrative (González 2002). I asked about this in the interview and he replied:

> I don't mention any of the miracles. There's one meaning of the Virgin that I want to recover. This has to do with her origin—the Virgin of Defense is defender of the peripheral and marginalized. There are two other meanings: one is almost mystical, which is

"defender of the little birds" [birds sheltered in the hermit's image in Father Orozco's account], and I think that miracles are involved in this meaning. There is another meaning that is "defender of ecclesiastical authority and of conquest. . . ." I leave aside these two meanings. I am interested in the meaning that has historical transcendence—that has real historical repercussion.

González appears to attribute agency to the Virgin as an active "defender of the peripheral and marginalized." However, when I asked him about this, he replied:

> She is the justification of many of the events. She doesn't have human functions and produce things. It's the social nuclei around her [that produce things].

That is a perfect example of what I mean by the secular perspective. Again, I am using the term "secular" in a broad sense for all histories that make a point of bracketing divine agency from the main frame of the narrative, even if they find another place for it. Martín González claims to champion "popular devotion" in the face of "ecclesiastical authority" but he distances himself from certain aspects of their devotion, bracketing the Virgin's own role, arguing that "a mystical, individualist devotion is not enough . . . it is important to sustain more and more the social meaning." Even though playing rhetorically with divine agency, González leaves that agency outside the main flow of the narrative, retelling what might otherwise be a narrative of miraculous intervention in purely human terms.

A Higher Ground: Knowing Secular History, Being Eminent Citizens?

Why did Tapalpans sometimes give secular histories of the Virgin of Defense despite their devotion to her? People in the Sierra were used to the idea that there was a secular "outside" of religion; it was possible to look in on religion as if from the outside. For example, Tapalpans were accustomed to the secular gaze of tourists' video cameras on their processions, and migrants on return visits from California had also begun to film the Virgin (illustration 22). In addition, the Mexican government had long forced its brand of political secularism upon the population. They prevented the clergy from voting, and (until 1992) running for office, registered them as federal employees and church buildings as federal property, and demanded that priests obey stringent rules and regulations for religious processions. The Church was prohibited from owning schools—religious orders continued to run schools but were forbidden from teaching Catholic doctrine. In other words, the religious field was subject to control from the outside; it was encompassed by the world of secular politics.

Secular history was also useful as a way to treat religious devotion in secular contexts. It allowed narrators to identify in certain respects with their devout subjects, while remaining "outside" in other respects. Narrators such as the authors of the *Monograph* could thus write of religious devotion within a secular context. They identified with their narrative subjects as residents of the Sierra but not, at least explicitly, as fellow devotees of the Virgin. Similarly, the municipal chronicler José Fajardo wrote several articles about the Virgin of Defense in his column in a regional newspaper. He used poetic language to aestheticize Tapalpans' devotion to the Virgin and to evoke his sympathy for their devotion, but he did not make explicit his own devotion to the Virgin in that secular context. Neither did he celebrate her miracles, any more than I did in my booklet on the Tapalpan church. Rather than lament the decline of religious devotion, he pleaded in one article that "it would be a lack of *historical sensibility* for memory to forget the celebration of San Antonio [the former patron saint of Tapalpa]" (Fajardo 1994; emphasis added).

Even when writing under the auspices of the Church, narrators such as Martín González and even priests gave secular histories. For one thing, it allowed Catholic narrators to reach a wider audience. González explained in his interview that he wanted to reach a wider audience than just the Virgin's faithful. He was anxious to draw the attention of politicians to the injustices of life in the Sierra de Tapalpa. His brand of theology was, as I have said, favored by the diocese. Liberation theology emphasizes human responsibility in a worldly struggle. In a sense, it does so precisely by bracketing (although not of course excluding) the next world. González focused on the struggle for social justice at the expense of the miracles featured in most talk about the Virgin.

I want to stress, though, that secular history offered a kind of higher ground or authority, rather as knowing Tapalpa's history offered a higher ground of cultura. The secular outside from which narrators looked in on the religious devotion of their protagonists was a special kind of higher ground.

On one occasion, for example, a Tapalpan man said that the Indians used to take the Virgin of Defense to visit hacienda owners who had threatened to take their lands; the owners would then forget their threats, and even join the processions. A friend from Guadalajara, Alfonso, replied that "it didn't work for them either" since everyone knew that the hacienda owners had ended up with all the lands. Perhaps because he was not a practicing Catholic, Alfonso found no place for the Virgin's agency, except in the deluded heads of the Indians who took the Virgin to win back their lands. He took an obviously higher ground, portraying the devoted as mistaken or misled and even manipulated by others. Academics and other intellectuals sometimes took a similar stance. The sociologist Jesús Tapia, a professor at El Colegio de Michoacán, wrote that the popular nineteenth-century cult of the Virgin of the Purest Conception in Zamora had been sponsored by the city's conservative bourgeoisie, as a response to liberal anticlericalism (Tapia Santamaría 1986). A Zamoran schoolteacher, Rafael, had read the article and asked what I thought about it. I said it was very good. He agreed, but added that *no se le puede quitar la fé al pueblo* (you can't take the people's faith away). Rafael was a devout Catholic but was also a high-school teacher with a bookish knowledge. He was often disdainful of popular beliefs and practices and most times took a higher ground. On this occasion, however, he felt the need to sympathize with "the people" and their devotion, which Tapia sought to scrutinize from the ground of academic social history (Stack 2007[a]).

I have said that knowing the Virgin's history was less obviously linked to citizenship than knowing Tapalpa's or Mexico's history, yet it did seem that secular history could add to the public voice and authority of eminent citizens. Being a Mexican citizen certainly meant setting religion aside in order, for example, to run for office; it is less clear that setting religion aside was necessary for being a citizen of Tapalpa (a focus of my current research). Nevertheless, there is some parallel between people's understandings of cultura and the higher ground of secular history. Briefly, if cultura involved the ability to apprehend that which lay beyond the immediate, secular history was a sign that narrators were not trapped in their immediate devotion. They were able to step outside to look in on religious devotion—their own and that of others—and to reflect on it, whether critically or otherwise. It allowed them to have devotion, just as they had rooting or belonging, without being confined by it. They could sympathize with and even identify with the devotion of others, as Fajardo did in Tapalpa and Rafael in Zamora, while choosing their moment to step outside that devotion and peer in on it. It allowed them to disparage others who remained confined within their devotion. The people of Atacco (and Juanacatlán) were accused not just of being trapped by present necessity and a lack of vision—selling their lands for a song or trading their votes for promised favors—but of practicing an unreflectively traditional brand of Catholicism that bordered on superstition. There was a sense, then, in which the secular perspective—including the ability to give a secular account of the Virgin's history—allowed people to claim a higher ground as good citizens and not just as enlightened Catholics.

Secular history, indeed, seemed to offer a sense of citizenship to priests, who were not even allowed to express an opinion on politics. Despite the government's restrictions, priests did still enjoy considerable status or authority in the Sierra de Tapalpa. They played a vital sacramental role in the lives of the faithful, of course, and many also drew on personal charisma to maintain a hold over them. But secular knowledge could offer them a further source of status or authority, to recover some of the authority that had been lost to secular politics. One strategy of the Church was to rely on Catholic lay leaders to participate and express the opinions that the clergy themselves were unable to. Leaders like Martín González, who played a significant role in the diocese, were to act, in a sense, as the Church's citizens by proxy; we have seen that he sought a wider audience for his history in order to highlight social injustice in the Sierra. But priests themselves, like Father Méndez, were known to produce secular history. Secular history was something that clerics could do well—don Lupe and Arámbula had referred me to Father Méndez's 1989 article on Tapalpa's history—benefiting, like Martín González, from the rigors of a seminary education and from ready access to parish archives, the principal source of Father Méndez's history. From the higher ground of the secular, priests could police what was known as "popular religiosity," scrutinizing the practices of the Virgin's faithful as if from the outside; I heard priests treat such practices much in the way of Fajardo or Rafael or of Jesús Tapia. But if priests could step outside their priestly role, displaying their own cosmopolitan credentials as bearers of cultura, it could only help them to maintain a place in broader public life—as eminent citizens, in the sense that I have used it throughout, albeit of a special kind. On the one hand, Tapalpans recalled the awesome hold on the faithful of Father Cipriano—a domineering parish priest of whom a statue has been built outside the parish church. Father Méndez's public role had been different than Father Cipriano's. One reason was that, unlike Father Cipriano, he was a native of Tapalpa. Another was that he could aspire to the broader horizons of cultura—a sign of which was history told from beyond faith—in a way that eluded the otherwise powerful Father Cipirano.

Histories of History

I have focused on people's notions of history during the 1990s, when I was doing fieldwork in and around the Sierra, for most of the book. However, I have mentioned histories written before then, including Father Orozco's published in 1954, and the *Monograph of Tapalpa* published in 1985. In the final part of the book, I offer what might be described as a history *of* history. Citizenship is less of a focus in the next two chapters but I end the third and final chapter by noting the history of history's links to citizenship.

PART IV

HISTORIES OF HISTORY

Tracing History and Histories Back in Time

CHAPTER EIGHT

Shifts in History

How a History Changes over Time

Dissatisfied with the task of rendering Tapalpa's history myself, I became interested in others' perceptions of history, and the book so far has focused on the histories told and written by others, mainly during my several periods of fieldwork between 1992 and 2005. In the final three chapters, though, I trace the history of these notions of history back in time, before 1992.

I have said more about people's ideas of what history is and why it is valuable than about what they actually told as history. I did mention, though, that I often heard Tapalpa was just a hacienda when Atacco was the pueblo. It was perhaps the one piece of history that most people knew and agreed upon. I will show that townspeople had not always given this account of how Tapalpa was founded—they gave a different account in the nineteenth century. So how did this account become so consensual by the end of the twentieth century? Scholars have written of how dominant or powerful groups impose their accounts of the past on others, and have linked different versions of history to the interests of different social groups (Nugent and Alonso 1994; Verdery 1993; Mallon 1995; Trouillot 1995; Appelbaum 2003). That is one of the ways in which I account for changes in Tapalpa's history. I observed in part II, for example, that landowning families in Tapalpa managed to portray themselves as "old" families, and I trace in this chapter how they came to pass themselves off as such in the first place, thus sidelining the Tapalpan Indians who were said in the nineteenth century to have founded the town. I also show that the post-Revolutionary government had an effect in shaping what was told as Tapalpa's history during the twentieth century, even if Tapalpans found it hard to connect Tapalpa's history with the Mexican history that they learned. However, I add a second approach to explaining the changes in Tapalpa's history. I described in part II how the skewing of history gave authority to some people over others, and helped to make some, such as don Lupe and Fajardo, into eminent citizens. In this chapter, I will note that people turned to those eminent citizens for history, which allowed them to shape, sometimes inadvertently, the history that others told and wrote. This skewing allowed not just don Lupe and Fajardo but also the "old" families—and the Mexican government—to mold what got told as Tapalpa's history.

I end the chapter by indicating that people turned to others not just for the particular history of Tapalpa's founding but for the genre of history itself—their understandings of what made for good history. It is not just the figure of Tapalpa's history that changes, indeed, but the ground of what is understood as history in the first place. I go on to sketch out in chapter 3 the broader history of the genre, which has developed in different ways at different times and places—hence the differences between talk of Tapalpa's history and Mexico's history and between history as it is told in Mexico, Scotland, and at Oxford and the University of Pennsylvania.

A *Shifting* History

Atacco was the town, when Tapalpa was a hacienda. That is what I heard over and over again, and from many different people. It was what most people said before referring me to someone else for a fuller account of Tapalpa's history. It was also why I was sent to Atacco in the first place. I have described what Atacco's antiquity meant to Federico's group, as well as to don Jorge's group and to Tapalpans.

I was surprised by a document that I read in the Tapalpa library: a municipal survey dated 1879, which included a section entitled "Founding." The survey was discovered in an archive a century later, and published in 1987 by Gabriel de Jesús Camarena y Gutiérrez de Laríz in a Guadalajara magazine (Camarena y Gutiérrez de Laríz 1987 [1879]). The 1879 survey had been written by two residents of Tapalpa, Camilo González and Manuel Cedeño. They began the survey by noting:

> The population of Tapalpa has its origin according to tradition, since data haven't been found, from a tribe of indigenous people from Zacoalco that, at the beginning of last century, came to tan hides, taking advantage of a raw material that was then abundant, the hawthorn bush, whose bark is one of the principal agents for tanning, as well as water. These indigenous people built the first shacks for living in; once settled, their population and progress began increasing. (24)

According to this history written in 1879, Tapalpa was founded not as a hacienda by Spaniards, as I was told in my fieldwork, but by indigenous people from a nearby town. The authors continued:

> That period saw the discovery of the silver and gold mines of El Rosario, San Rafael, San José del Amparo, El Realito, La Guadalupe, El Palo Alto, and other seams that many Spaniards and Creoles came to exploit; and when the principal mine San Rafael was in decline, all those miners emigrated to Tapalpa, where they settled as *vecinos* [neighbors or residents], among the indigenous people, from whom for the most part their children descend. (24)

The indigenous Zacoalcans were, then, not left for long on their own but were joined by Spanish and Creole ex-miners. In the third paragraph, the authors wrote:

> The town of San Gaspar de Atlanco, whose original name has today mutated into that of Atacco, already existed, and was the county seat, formed of pure indigenous people who received their conqueror Pedro de Alvarado. (24–25)

This did sound more like what I heard during my fieldwork. The conqueror Pedro de Alvarado was not mentioned and people did not use the name San Gaspar de Atlanco. But I was told repeatedly that Atacco was considered older than Tapalpa, had a higher civic status originally, and was inhabited by

Indians. I discuss that continuity in the next chapter, while in this chapter I focus on the changes in what was told of Tapalpa's history.

The Elision of Indians

The 1879 account is a written document, but I argue that it still gives us an idea of what people were saying in 1879. First, the authors begin by claiming that they drew on "tradition" rather than "datos" [data]—they clearly meant information transmitted orally as opposed to written documents. They would have cited written documents if they could, especially in an official survey for bureaucrats. The author of the 1879 survey of the nearby town of Sayula, for example, stressed that he was relying on written documents (González 1971 [1879], 4). Second, I have not found any likely written source for their account of Tapalpa's founding so the authors do genuinely seem to have drawn a blank.

It seems, then, that people stopped saying, at some point between 1879 and 1992, that Tapalpa was settled first by Indians and later by Spaniards and Creoles, while still saying that Atacco was older and an Indian town. It is no easy task to trace the disappearance of the idea that Tapalpa was settled first by Indians. I said in part II that the Atacco group had trouble finding enough evidence for their town's history, as well as knowing what to make of the evidence that they did find. Don Lupe had warned me off looking for documentary evidence. What follows is partly guesswork, but I did have better access to documents than the Atacco group, and perhaps a better sense of what to make of what I found.

To begin with, it is likely that Tapalpans in 1879 talked of the Indian residents' responsibility for a chapel in the town center, but by 1902 it was no longer associated with them. The authors of the 1879 survey wrote that "Tapalpan Indians" were charged with the upkeep of the Purísima chapel that faced the old parish church (Camarena y Gutiérrez de Laríz 1987 [1879]). An earlier document in the parish archive also described their role in rebuilding that chapel (APT Libro de Gobierno 3:241). Father Méndez did say in his 1987 article that it had been the Indians' chapel, and Arámbula also made the connection when we talked in 1992. But I have heard nothing else on the subject and there is no later document that makes the association. Significantly, a resident in 1999 linked the chapel to the last owner of the Hacienda de Buenavista, Vidal Vizcaíno. It was the chapel of the hacienda,

Illustration 24: Tombs of the hacienda owner, Vidal Vizcaíno, buried in 1902 next to his first wife, in the Purisima Chapel, previously in the care of Tapalpa's indigenous community (2005).

he added. Vidal Vizcaíno and his first wife were buried in 1902 before the altar in the chapel, and the tombstones were very visible (illustration 24). I think it probable that soon after 1879 Tapalpa's indigenous community ceased to take care of the chapel, and that after 1902 people gradually came to associate it with Vidal Vizcaíno instead. That removed one reason for people to speak of "Tapalpan Indians."

People would have also talked about Tapalpan Indians in relation to land disputes in the nineteenth century, but being Indian was no longer relevant to local land disputes by the early twentieth century. I found a series of documents indicating that people were still trying to claim lands in the name of an "indigenous community of Tapalpa" during the 1860s and 1870s (Colección de Acuerdos 1868, 349; 1879, 257–58). Some lands were in fact given by the municipal council to "indigenous people" in 1871, presumably in response to a federal law that pushed municipal governments to distribute lands to indigenous peoples (Vanderwood 1998, 72). However, the grant was not made to an "indigenous community," but simply to the "neediest indigenous persons" (Colección de Acuerdos 1879, 44–45). Indeed, one of these documents refers in 1874 to the "extinct indigenous community" (367–68). No land claims by indigenous persons or an indigenous community were mentioned anywhere in the 1879 survey. In the 1920s, I have said that Atacco residents changed their land claim from "restitution" of the lands of their "ancient town" to "endowment" of lands on the grounds of present needs. Tapalpan activists applied in 1932 for an "endowment" of land (ASRA 181:17 and 564). By then it made no sense to claim lands in the name of an "indigenous community."

While Tapalpa's Indians were disappearing from talk, others were keen to present themselves as "old" families of Tapalpa. I found during my fieldwork that some Tapalpan families showed particular interest in the idea that Atacco was the town when Tapalpa was a hacienda. For example, Manuel Preciado, an elderly resident born in Tapalpa in 1910, said in 1993 that his family had been one of the first to settle in Tapalpa after the building of the hacienda. Around that time, he said, the county seat moved to Tapalpa. He and his sisters had learned this history from their father, also born in Tapalpa. It is not hard to guess why their father had wanted to claim that their family was among Tapalpa's founders: being an "old" family would have given them a claim against "new" families. The authors of the 1879 survey, González and Cedeño, considered Indians to be Tapalpa's founders but they did write that some Spanish and Creole miners had later settled among them—and thus had some claim to be "old" families if not the first ones. No doubt González and Cedeño considered the Preciado family to be one of these "old" families, since there were many Preciados in Tapalpa in 1879, they owned lands at the time (as they do now), claimed Spanish descent, and were closely linked to the Vizcaíno family who owned the Hacienda de Buenavista. Who were the "new" families from which such families wished to distinguish themselves? I mentioned in part I that several families came to Tapalpa in the revolutionary years to exploit opportunities opened by the departure of such elite families as the Vizcainos and doña Carmen's—in fact, the Preciados were one of the few such families to stay. Don Manuel and his sisters recalled their father's anger at the immigrant Spaniards who, as I mentioned in part I, came to Tapalpa in 1915 and tried to take over the logging industry. Others lamented the arrival in the 1920s of the Alcaraz family from the Sierra del Tigre, who took the municipal presidency by force, before eventually being exiled from the town. The case of the Manzanos was more ambiguous because they moved from Atacco but they were still new to Tapalpa. So the Preciados pushed their claim to be an "old" family against these presumptuous "new" families. As the years went by, it seems that their claim prospered—all the more so as people turned to them, as an "old" family, for the town's history.

By the 1940s, it appears that some Tapalpans were saying that their town was settled first by families of Spanish descent, like the Preciados. Father Méndez, the priest native to Tapalpa whom we encountered in part III, also came from a family who claimed Spanish descent and held lands around Tapalpa. Significantly, he wrote in his 1948 history of the Virgin of Defense that there was little strife at the time of conquest in the region and that "there were cases like that of Atacco in which the Spaniard was allowed to settle alone in Tapalpa" (Mendez 1948, 11). It is likely that he lifted his claim that "the Spaniard was allowed to settle alone in Tapalpa" from what some people, at least, were saying in the 1940s. He refers to documents in support of the other points of his history, but he does not do so for this point, which suggests that he heard it spoken rather than read it; residents also remembered that the priest used to take notes from conversations. Whether people were already saying it or not, Father Méndez's claim was no doubt taken up by others, since he was greatly respected. His history circulated at the time in Tapalpa (although there were very few copies left by 1992). More importantly, the same priest returned frequently to Tapalpa and he was happy to talk of Tapalpa's history when visiting the town.

A careful comparison of the two narratives—that of 1879 and what I heard during my fieldwork—gives another clue about the elision of Indians from Tapalpa's history. Figure 1 illustrates the ethnic groups identified by the 1879 survey. The population of Atacco, represented as I_1, had always been there. Tapalpa was settled in two waves: first by Indians from a lowland town, represented by I_2 and the bold arrow, and second by Spaniards and Creoles from nearby mines, represented by S and the lighter arrow. They write of the Spaniards and Creoles "settling among" among the earlier Indian settlers "from whom their children descend." It might seem, then, that Tapalpa had become a *mestizo* (mixed-blood) town. However, when the authors in a later section classify the population of the county, they divide it into two groups of about 3,500 each, one of "indigenous race" and the other of "white race," and then list a third but much smaller group of about 350 individuals who were "descended from both races." In other words, they considered very few people to be the mestizo produce of Spaniards and Creoles settling among the Indians.

By contrast, I found that most Tapalpans from 1992 to 2005 considered themselves and most others to be mestizo, and that was reflected in what people said of Tapalpa's history. Figure 2 maps out the ethnic groups who featured in what people told as Tapalpa's history from 1992 to 2005. When residents said in 1992 that "Atacco was the town, Tapalpa was the hacienda," they sometimes followed this by saying that people came from Atacco to work on the hacienda and then built their houses around its core. Like the history given in 1879, it was a history of mestizaje—of how Tapalpa became a mestizo town. But it was a different kind of mestizaje, as revealed by a comparison of figures 1 and 2. In the 1992 history, the only Indians (marked with an I) were the Indians of Atacco who had not yet moved to Tapalpa, leaving their Indian-ness behind. There was no room for Tapalpan Indians—they were squeezed out of the picture. As more and more people labeled themselves and others as mestizos, the idea that Tapalpa was founded by Indians receded until it was left only in documents.

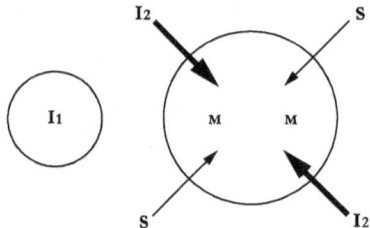

Figure 1. Ethnicity in Tapalpa's history in the 1879 survey.

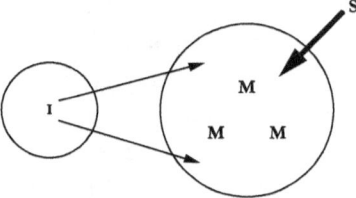

Figure 2. Ethnicity in Tapalpa's history as told in 1992–2005.

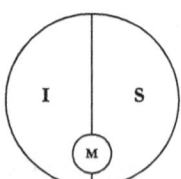

Figure 3. Dominant view of Mexican society in the nineteenth century.

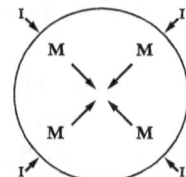

Figure 4. Dominant view of Mexican society after the Revolution.

I = Indian (in figure 1, I_1 = first group of Indians; I_2 = second group of Indians); M = Mestizo; S = Spanish or Creole.

The 1990s version of mestizaje—Indians leaving their Indianness behind—was likely shaped by decades of propaganda from the post-Revolutionary Mexican state. I observed in part III that people did not often connect what they said of Mexican history with what they said of Tapalpan history, which was why the two histories could exist side-by-side without having much contact with one other. I have also noted that there was resistance to state propaganda, especially with regard to the land reform. I described in part I the support of some Tapalpans for the Cristero rebels in the 1920s, and Tapalpan landowners forged an alliance with the parish priest Father Cipriano, which helped them to frustrate the attempts of Tapalpan peasants to establish an ejido. However, state propaganda did make some inroads in the Sierra, not least because the same landowners became stalwarts of the governing PRI and learned to navigate the "vertical" structures set up after the Revolution. Meanwhile, municipal and parish schools were replaced by state government schools, exposing many children to the post-Revolutionary textbooks (Friedlander 1975; Palacios 1999; Vaughan 1997). So it is not surprising that some themes of official Mexican history did find their way into what was told of Tapalpa's history, most obviously the post-Revolutionary account of mestizaje. Figure 3 illustrates dominant notions of Mexican society in the nineteenth century. Government surveys tended to divide the population into those of Spanish descent (S) and Indians (I), together with a smaller group identified as mestizo (M). That corresponds closely to González and Cedeño's description of Tapalpa's ethnic groups in 1879. Figure 4 shows the post-Revolutionary government's vision of the nation. Mexico was a mestizo nation, the revolutionaries argued, but not just in the sense that there was more and more intermarriage. For José Vasconcelos, the pioneering education minister of the 1920s, Mexico was the stage for a racial fusion of Spaniards and Indians that was giving birth to a "cosmic race," and many Mexicans continue to present themselves as mestizos in terms of race or blood (Vasconcelos 1979 [1925]). Other ideologues preferred to view mestizaje as a fusion of cultures but one in which the indigenous heritage was largely kept to performance in villages and exhibits in museums, where it would not obstruct Mexico's modernization (Friedlander 1975). Either way, being Indian came to mean being on the periphery of modern Mexico, rather than just being the poorer half of the population. The resemblance between figures 2 and 4—between that post-Revolutionary vision of Mexico and what was told of Tapalpa's history by the 1990s—is striking. Having narrated in 1879 the history of a Tapalpa founded by the fusion of two groups, Tapalpans were saying by the 1990s that the only Indians were those in Atacco—peripheral to Tapalpa—who had not yet moved to the more modern town. Even in Atacco, I cited don Alfredo's comment during the Federico group's meeting: although Atacco was "the oldest of Tapalpa and of all these towns around here ... we went there [to Tapalpa] and made it bigger, abandoning this town, and the governments we've had are always leaving it behind, behind, behind, and it remains in poverty."

The Rise of the Hacienda

I have said that I was told during my fieldwork that Tapalpa was founded as a hacienda, presumably by Spaniards. More precisely, many people did say, when prompted, that Spaniards must have founded the hacienda, but not all volunteered this and a few were not so sure. In other words, people said in 1879 that Tapalpa was founded by Indians, but by 1992 most people stressed instead the kind of settlement that Tapalpa had once been.

How did the idea that Tapalpa was founded as a hacienda manage to take over its history between 1879 and 1992? To begin with, whereas it seems that people ceased talking of Tapalpan Indians after they no longer held lands or took care of the chapel, they continued to talk about the hacienda even after its demise. In the 1990s much of this talk concerned the bittersweet experience of hacienda life—the security on the one hand and the harsh conditions on the other. But land disputes from the 1920s onward often referred back to the extensive lands of the hacienda that were redistributed among the ejidos in the Sierra. A handful of activists in Tapalpa were still looking in the 1990s for documents about ownership of the hacienda. Physical location was the most obvious link of the hacienda to the town itself. The main house of the hacienda on the corner of Tapalpa's plaza was demolished in the 1960s, but the hotel built in its place was called the Hotel Hacienda. During my fieldwork, residents often pointed to the central location of this hotel as evidence that Tapalpa was indeed a hacienda (illustrations 25 and 26).

Among local residents, two groups had a special interest in the idea that Tapalpa was a hacienda, and both groups were seen as authorities on the town's history. Some Tapalpan landowners liked to celebrate their connections to the hacienda and its wealthy owners. The Preciado family made reference to the hacienda in the 1990s, saying that they settled in Tapalpa shortly after the hacienda was built. The older Preciados liked to tell about how they were part of the social circle of the hacienda owners, and were invited to play as children in the hacienda. A second interested group was Atacco's residents, for whom the idea that Tapalpa was just a hacienda when Atacco was a pueblo served to reinforce the point that their town was older and had been more important—it was "the most founded town" in don Alfredo's words. The idea that Tapalpa was a hacienda was also taken up and reproduced by Tapalpa's historians, the authoritative individuals that I have discussed. None of them wrote of the hacienda until the 1990s, but I found in 1992 that don Lupe and others said in conversation that Tapalpa was founded as a hacienda, even if they did not say the same in their written histories.

Illustration 25: Vidal Vizcaíno's son contemplates the Hacienda de Buenavista in ruins before its demolition in the 1960s (photo courtesy of Sra. Consuelo de la Torre).

Illustration 26: View of the location of the old Hacienda de Buenavista from La Villa bar in the corner of Tapalpa's plaza (2005). The main sign on the balcony reads "Artesanías La Hacienda" (a shop that sells artisanal products, with the same owners as the Hotel Hacienda).

The idea of the hacienda was resonant far beyond Tapalpa, which helps to explain why people were so persuaded that Tapalpa had been a hacienda. A Guadalajaran observed in 2005 that she was amazed at how many towns seemed to have originated as haciendas; traveling around, I found that people in many towns played up the rise and fall of haciendas in the histories of their towns. Tapalpans found the same when they traveled to other towns, which appears to have convinced them that the hacienda was a likely origin for Tapalpa, too. State propaganda and the heritage industry seem to have turned the hacienda into a staple of small-town history. Along with the ideology of mestizaje, the post-Revolutionary state prided itself on having broken the power of the haciendas; floats, textbooks, and agrarian talk from the 1930s deployed the hacienda as a counterfoil for the Revolution (Vaughan 1997; Benjamin 2000). That propaganda seems to have led people to think of the hacienda as a piece of history, even in towns such as Tapalpa where the hacienda was seen more positively (Uzeta 1997). In recent years, haciendas have featured in movies and in telenovelas, as I will mention, and have been advertised in glossy magazines as sites for society weddings, weekend getaways, and so on. That Tapalpa had been a hacienda had an obvious allure for tourism—Atacco may have been the pueblo, but Tapalpa was the kind of place in which you could spend your weekends in seigniorial splendor—but it also had a clear appeal for some of the town's residents.

Illustration 27: In 1999 the organizers of the Independence Day celebrations decided to include a parade commemorating Tapalpa's history on the day before the main parades. Only one of the floats made any obvious reference to Tapalpa's history: a cart, hauled by oxen, bearing the name Hacienda de Buenavista.

Shifting Grounds of History

In much of the book I have described the genre of history as if it were set in stone. I ended part I by linking history to the kind of truth that is produced through public debate; in part II, I linked public debate to the quality of cultura and the citizenship of towns. But the intricate connections between history, cultura, citizenship, and towns were always shifting, even from one day to another and from one person to another. The same was true of the relations between different strains of history, such as the history told for weekenders and by migrants, and of the relation between the history of towns and national history, as I described in part III, and between secular and nonsecular histories of the Virgin. Even the most local shifts in the ground of history were tied into broader shifts. One reason why Tapalpa's history changed during the twentieth century was that people's outlook was shaped increasingly by the Mexican state, which happened to be disseminating its idea of mestizaje and casting the hacienda as a foil for its Revolution. The state gave an impetus to the idea of history itself, mainly through schooling. I suspect that few people in 1879 were well acquainted with the genre of history; if people were saying that Atacco was older, they were not necessarily saying this as history, even if González and Cedeño were.

It is possible to trace shifts in different strains of history even through the period of my fieldwork. For example, Fajardo began teaching the diploma classes in 2004 and by 2005 his students were introducing fragments of written history into what they said of Tapalpa's history. At the same time, Fajardo picked up on ideas of history from his teacher, José María Muriá, who in turn had engaged with wider ideas about local and regional history, especially those of Luis González y González. It is not surprising, then, that Fajardo began during the 1990s to refer to the oral accounts of elderly men and women, as González y González had done. Muriá had promoted the teaching of regional history in schools and, during my fieldwork, school pupils were studying the history of Jalisco alongside Mexican history. Meanwhile, business owners were more interested in using Tapalpa's history as part of the town's tourist image, trying to develop a style of history that could lend itself to glossy leaflets and television spots, and drawing on technical support from the Pueblos Mágicos federal program. The Catholic Church had long promoted history, publishing Father Méndez's 1948 history and Father Orozco's in 1954, but the diocese of Ciudad Guzmán came to promote a style of history that played up the struggle for social justice, of which Martín González's history of the Virgin of Defense (2002) was a fine example.

In the remaining two chapters, however, I will point to some of the similarities and continuities in the history told of Tapalpa and the genre of history itself. They demonstrate, I will argue, the enduring success of history.

CHAPTER NINE

A Successful History

What Did Not Change

The previous chapter was all about change—the remaining two chapters are about continuity. I have just traced how the history told of Tapalpa's founding changed during the twentieth century, but here I show that one crucial piece of that history did not change.

González and Cedeño wrote in 1879 that Atacco "already existed and was the principal town, made up of pure indigenous people," and in 1992 people still stressed that Atacco was (already) the town when Tapalpa was founded (Camarena y Gutiérrez de Laríz 1987 [1879], 24–25). That might seem a faithful reflection of the historical fact that Atacco was older, but suffice it to say that Tapalpa and Atacco are both listed as "Indian towns" in the first census conducted by the Spaniards, the 1548 *Suma de Visitas*. It might also seem like a simple case of inertia—the idea that Atacco was already the town survived in spite of far-reaching changes in the social context. But, following Greg Urban's work (2001), I find that inertia is not a sufficient explanation. The idea that "Atacco was the town" was carried through the period on the back of the interests of different groups and of the authority of the individuals to whom people turned for their history.

I begin this chapter by trying to explain how the idea that Atacco was the town endured from 1879 to 1992. It is partly guesswork, again, and I go on to focus on the period of my fieldwork, from 1992 to 2005, when I could observe the transmission of history at close quarters. I look more closely at the agreement among Tapalpans about this history. Rather than take this consensus for granted, I ask why so many different people gave such a similar history, and kept doing so from 1992 to 2005.

Atacco was the Town, 1879–1992

How does one explain the persistence of the idea, from 1879 to 1992, that Atacco was older than Tapalpa? It is no easy task. For one thing, the idea was transmitted through diffuse channels, which are hard to reconstruct. There was no single source to which people turned between 1879 and 1992. I have mentioned, for example, that the 1879 survey seems to have gathered dust in an archive in Guadalajara and was not cited in print until the 1980s. Neither was Tapalpa's history offered in schools (and regional history was not taught until the 1980s). That makes it hard to explain the reproduction of this history, and it also makes it difficult to trace.

Tapalpa's elites, while pushing a new history that foregrounded Tapalpa's "old" Spanish families and the place of the hacienda, remained interested throughout the period in the idea that Atacco was older, especially because it served to set in relief a modern, progressive Tapalpa. I said in the previous chapter that there was some uptake from Mexico's history into what was told of Tapalpa's history, even if Tapalpa's history was otherwise quite insulated. We have seen that post-Revolutionary propaganda introduced the new idea of mestizaje as well as using the emblem of the hacienda; it continued with the nineteenth-century accent on progress. González and Cedeño were keen to play up Tapalpa's progressiveness in the 1879 report, and the idea that Atacco was older helped them by setting Tapalpa's progress in relief. The image of Tapalpa as a progressive place was important to the town's elite. González had successfully petitioned the state government in 1878 to raise Tapalpa's civic status from pueblo to villa (a status between pueblo and city) on the grounds of its progress and potential. That accounts for the celebratory tone of the 1879 survey, which they had titled "Villa de Tapalpa" even though it was supposed to represent the whole municipal district (Camarena y Gutiérrez de Laríz 1987 [1879]). In another section of the survey, the authors locate only "traditional" industries (such as cactus-fiber crafts) in Atacco, as opposed to the modern industries and mining that they linked to Tapalpa

Illustration 28: The municipal council marching in the Independence Day parade in Tapalpa (1999). The council included several members of "old" families.

(42–45). Tapalpa's elite continued after 1879 to show Tapalpa's progress, and continued to use Atacco to set Tapalpa in relief. The idea of progress was evident in the few municipal records from the 1930s. Successive presidents claimed to champion the literacy campaigns, for example. Father Méndez in 1948 was quick to contrast Tapalpa's development and promise against Atacco's backwardness. On some occasions, locals were found wanting, such as when an agrarian inspector issued a damning report on Atacco residents in 1954.

Atacco's relative antiquity was of interest to its own residents throughout the period, although the reasons for their interest changed. Two elderly Atacco men, who were born in the town, said in 1995 that they had always heard that Atacco was older, including from the old people when they were young, but documentary sources suggest that it was of interest for different reasons at different times. In the nineteenth century and in the early twentieth century, it was of interest because an ancient town still had rights to lands. But I noted in the previous chapter that the right of "indigenous towns" to land had been eroded by the early twentieth century, and paradoxically, by the agrarian reform of the 1920s. I mentioned that a group of agrarian activists from Atacco applied in 1921 for a "restitution" of the lands of their "ancient town." Seemingly in support of the application, in 1923 one of the activists copied a land title that, among other things, contrasted the "old town" of Atacco with the "new town" of Tapalpa. As I explained, the post-Revolutionary government agreed instead to make an "endowment" of lands simply on the grounds that they were peasants in need of lands to farm (Craig 1983, 249–51). That made Atacco's antiquity legally irrelevant, at least with regard to claiming lands. However, Atacco residents had another reason to claim antiquity—as a mark of civic status. Atacco's civic status was already mentioned in the 1879 survey: Atacco had been not just a town but the *cabecera* (county seat). I described in part II the struggle of Federico's group to reclaim Atacco's civic status in the face of Tapalpans' contempt. In doing so, the group found themselves in conflict with don Jorge's group, which had unearthed the 1923 copy of the land title to claim lands for Atacco as, once again, an ancient indigenous town.

I have mentioned that there was no central source that might explain the remarkable resilience of the idea that Atacco was the town. The 1879 survey was buried in an archive. However, there was some skewing—people turned to certain authoritative persons and groups for their history. It is likely that the survey authors were one such source. They did at least remain prominent in the town—Camilo González became municipal president in 1902 and José Cedeño was remembered as wealthy, although they each had died or left Tapalpa by the 1930s. It is difficult to show that people turned to the "old" families, although we have seen that the Preciado family did at least talk to each other about Tapalpa's history. Some people certainly turned to Atacco residents—Alberto Arámbula had talked with his Atacco laborers and paid attention to their history (while discussing documents that he had found or heard about). By the 1980s Arámbula himself was giving talks on Tapalpa's history and people were asking him about it. The same was true of Father Méndez, and it is significant that Father Méndez wrote in 1948 that the people of Atacco had decided who could settle in Tapalpa. Atacco had, in his influential account, certainly been the older and more senior town.

Atacco Was the Town, 1992–2005

Although anthropologists have paid attention to change within the ethnographic present, they have largely taken for granted continuity during the same period. Given that the idea of Atacco's antiquity persisted from 1879 to 1992, moreover, it might seem unsurprising that the idea was still relevant in 2005. Rather than take the continuity for granted, however, I will try to explain it.

I began part I by introducing my landlady, Teresa, whom I met in 1992 shortly after arriving in Tapalpa. Five years later, when I returned to do my PhD fieldwork, I had grown close to her, which meant among other things that I liked to argue with her. On one occasion, for example, I said while she was making the main meal of the day, that Tapalpa, like its neighbor Atacco, had been a *pueblo indio* (Indian town). Teresa agreed, tentatively, that this was possible, even referring at one point to the Indians of Tapalpa as "us." She said, however, that the people of both Atacco and Juanacatlán, another nearby town, were more Indian than the people of Tapalpa. She was open to my suggestion that different groups of Indians had lived in Atacco and Tapalpa. I pointed out that most Tapalpans said, by contrast, that Tapalpa had first settled as a hacienda by Spaniards, and I emphasized that this implied that no one had lived there prior to that time. She volunteered that, after all, the Spanish settlers could hardly have built their large houses by themselves. I suggested that the laborers could have come from neighboring Atacco. She did not respond. The idea of Spanish settlers living among Indians in Tapalpa and marrying them reminded her of her Spanish grandfather. He, she said, had married a woman "from here," very Indian and tall, with dark eyes. I asked whether Tapalpa looked like a pueblo indio: she began by contrasting the outgoing municipal president with his white skin and green eyes to the "very Indian" incoming president. I asked about the architecture and she said that Tapalpa did not look as "Indianized" as Atacco. There were more modern houses in Juanacatlán than in Atacco, she conceded. But the people of Juanacatlán were still Indian—and spoke as such—despite their houses. And so on.

Just as Teresa stuck to her story despite my attempts to shift her perspective, I found that many others kept saying, through the period, that Tapalpa had been a hacienda while its neighbor Atacco was the town. Not just people who had resided for many years in Tapalpa, but most people who had spent any significant time there. For example, in early 1998 a white-goods salesman, who had lived for only a few years in Tapalpa, told me he had heard from friends that Atacco was older than Tapalpa. "I didn't believe it," he said, "but it's true." I also heard much the same in Atacco, albeit with slightly different inflections.

Again, I found it surprising that "Atacco was the town" survived through the social changes of 1992 to 2005. Just as for the period 1879 to 1992, there was little institutional control over the transmission of Tapalpa's history. Parents did not sit their children down to tell them this history; it was not played out ritually or narrated in public gatherings; there were no plaques on the town square; and it was not taught in schools, although pupils were required to write projects on local history. As I explained in part I, residents did not even find history particularly interesting—their attention would turn quickly to more immediate concerns, such as children or gossip. So Tapalpa's history was transmitted through sporadic encounters among a population that was dispersed—many long-term residents left for Guadalajara and also for California while weekenders, teachers, bureaucrats, and others came and went. The diffuse transmission of Tapalpa's history made it difficult to trace and to explain.

It was also surprising that the idea that Atacco was the town survived when the bulk of written accounts, to which people did sometimes refer, appeared to undermine it. My explanation is that people only rarely engaged with what was written when they were speaking. On the one hand, Tapalpans tended to reproduce what others had written then they were writing history themselves. I found that most written histories were lifted almost word for word from other written histories. One example was the *Monograph of Tapalpa*, which I was handed in the town library:

> Tapalpa: Means place situated high up, which sits very well on account of its Geographical situation; in antiquity this Town was a small *Cacicazgo* [pre-Hispanic chiefdom] belonging to the Tlatonazgo of Tzoallan. (Nava López et al. 1985, 2)

Browsing further in the library's archive, I realized that the author had lifted this section word for word from another library handout. This other handout was typed in turn from the 1954 book by Father Orozco, the priest from Guadalajara that I cited in part III. On the other hand, if most wrote what was written, I found that only a few people drew on what was written when talking about "history." I felt I was doing good history in my conversation with Teresa by appealing to the evidence of documents, including the ones cited in the previous chapter as well as others cited in the 1989 magazine article written by Father Méndez. It was clear to me from those documents that Tapalpa had existed prior to the hacienda (and indeed, to the Conquest) and that an "indigenous community of Tapalpa" still existed in the late nineteenth century. Father Méndez's article was easily accessible and was read by several Tapalpans in the 1990s; the *Monograph of Tapalpa*, which was handed out to anyone who asked in the library about Tapalpa's history, also appeared to indicate that Tapalpa had been an Indian town. People referred to the existence of these writings in talk but seldom made use of the content in their conversation about history. I myself wrote that Tapalpa had been settled originally by Indians—and not an eyebrow was raised by my readers. The same was true of the 1879 survey that I described in the previous chapter. People had read it and sometimes cited it in their writings but did not incorporate it into their spoken histories of Tapalpa. That helps to explain why people kept saying that Atacco was older in the face of the documentary evidence.

So why did Teresa respond at all to my argument? One reason was that I was a history graduate, which gave me some authority, but I also went out of my way to insist on the point in a way that she could not easily ignore. I emphasized the fact that most people said or implied that no one had lived in Tapalpa before the hacienda, whereas, I continued, I had found evidence in written documents that there were Indians living in Tapalpa before the Spanish arrived. Despite that, she was clearly reluctant to take my history seriously. During further visits between 1999 and 2004, I made a similar point in many conversations with different people. I received a range of responses, but most expressed surprise at my argument and took some persuading. I had to persevere and was made to defend my argument, citing documents and brandishing my authority. I had a similar experience with the residents of Atacco. So why were all these people so reluctant to accept my revised history?

Interests

Most Tapalpan residents gave a negative spin to the idea that "Atacco was the town." Tapalpans often spoke of the "backwardness" of Atacco's residents, which resonated with the idea that Atacco had been eclipsed by Tapalpa. The events during my fieldwork that I outlined in part I did nothing to counter those prejudices. The growth in electoral competition, for example, served only to reinforce the distinction between the towns. Tapalpans complained after municipal elections in 1994 and in 1997 that the "Indians of Atacco" had voted for the incumbent PRI out of ignorance. Competition over resources was part of what was at stake—Tapalpans complained that the PRI municipal president, Arnoldo Zamora, spent the budget in places like Atacco rather than in Tapalpa. Curiously, though, some Tapalpans in the municipal government proposed in 2005 that Atacco deserved an increase in spending because it was older.

Among Tapalpan residents, some families showed particular interest in the idea that Atacco was the town when Tapalpa was a hacienda. I began part II by noting that some families in the 1990s were considered "old," or at least more obviously "from here" than other families. Again, this history gave those families a place in Tapalpa's founding: it was easier to claim antiquity in a "new" place. For example, Manuel Preciado was able to stake a claim for his family in this history of Tapalpa. He died in 1994, but at least one of his sons and other younger relatives have shown an interest in this history. Meanwhile, I noted in part II that Atacco's residents kept stressing that Atacco was in fact older—they were one group that was particularly interested. Some said that "Atacco used to be the town" when complaining about being sidelined from the municipal government. Atacco residents continued to tell the same history throughout this period. Some like don Jorge were indignant, indeed, that the *Monograph* and other documents appeared to deny that Atacco was older—or made scant mention of Atacco.

Skewing

Just as for the period 1879 to 1992, there was no institutional control over Tapalpa's history, but people did still turn to certain authoritative persons and groups, which included those having the most interest in the idea that Atacco was older. First, as described in part I, I was sent to talk to the *viejitos* (old people) in and around the center of Tapalpa in the 1990s. It was only later that I realized that they were not just old people, but were old people considered to be from "old" families. I did not hear them called that often, but when I asked other residents for Tapalpa's oldest families, many named don Manuel Preciado's family, in particular, as one of the oldest. Atacco's residents had still more obvious authority over the history being transmitted, even if Atacco's antiquity was sometimes read as a sign of backwardness. In fact, some members of the "old" families had also talked history with the people of Atacco—who often worked for them, held lands adjoining their own or were otherwise linked to them.

Those known for their historical knowledge—don Lupe and others—also tended to reproduce the idea that Atacco was older, at least in their spoken history. Unlike most other residents, don Lupe, Fajardo, Arámbula, and others were concerned to produce histories that conformed to the norms of good history, especially by citing a wide range of sources including written documents. Nevertheless, most of them still—especially in spoken history—made the same distinction between Tapalpa and Atacco, albeit with variations of their own. They did so sometimes by citing what they had heard. For example, Arámbula cited "tradition" in a talk on Tapalpa's history he gave in 1985, and had obviously spoken with Atacco residents—he had adjoining lands and several had worked and talked with him—and he was also close to the "old" families of Tapalpa.

Resonance

It was not just that a few people kept saying that Atacco was the town. The history was more successful than that—almost everyone seemed to give the same history, right from 1992 through to 2005. How does one explain its popularity? To begin with, the idea that Atacco was the town already had critical mass by 1992. When the salesman said, "I didn't believe it, but it's true," he was persuaded eventually because he found that so many people said the same thing about Tapalpa's history. To become that familiar, it needed to be heard often. I noted in part I, however, that most other Tapalpans did not find history particularly interesting, but I also noted that they would give tokens of history. "Atacco was the town while Tapalpa was a hacienda" was the token statement repeated by most people. I suggest it worked especially well as a token of history because it was a neat couplet. Atacco was the town, Tapalpa was a hacienda. Atacco was the town also worked as a token of history because it resonated with so much else going on in the period. It resonated with jokes, for instance: Teresa often laughed about the fact that I visited Atacco so often, warning me not to return too drunk. It was not just Teresa who joked about the people of Atacco—most people did who had lived for any length of time in Tapalpa, including some with holiday houses in the area. Finally, the idea that Atacco was the town resonated with things said and done beyond the Sierra. People moved from town to town, just as I did, and picked up elements of the history of other towns, whether from talk or from plaques of various kinds. Not surprisingly, Tapalpa's history did look remarkably like what was told as the history of other towns. I have said that haciendas were a common feature in the history of towns. Traveling around Mexico, I found that the history told of towns usually also followed the same template: this town X was founded in Y year by people of Z ethnicity. There were even other pairs of neighboring Indian and non-Indian towns. This also helps to explain why newcomers found it easy to pick up Tapalpa's history. "Atacco was the town when Tapalpa was a hacienda" was a familiar enough history to most people.

A Successful History, the Success of History

The success of this particular history owed something, then, to the wider success of the genre of history. By genre I mean not just the idea of the past and of public debate, the canons of evidence, and the link to cultura and rooting, but also themes and motifs, such as the hacienda, and whole plot structures, such as the idea that some places are older than others (White 1973, 1987).

The genre of history has been a success far beyond Mexico. It is true that there were differences between ideas of history in Tapalpa and, say, Oxford. I began the book by noting that Tapalpans were slower to play off their town history against Mexican history than I had expected. Another difference was that history at Oxford was concerned with important events, about which Tapalpans were less worried. The Oxford historian quoted in part I was more dubious of oral sources than don Lupe and others. Would other historians be able to check and make their own use of my data? Would my cassettes be available to other historians? Nevertheless, I have hinted throughout that there were many similiarites between Tapalpan ideas of history and those that I had learned at Oxford and previously at school in Scotland. I have suggested, too, that there has been an association between history and towns in the United Kingdom, and in California—where I did fieldwork on Tapalpan migrants and later on citizenship. Not only did most Californian towns and cities have historical associations, but their members dedicated extraordinary amounts of time and energy to them.

CHAPTER TEN

The Success of History

How a Genre Prospers

I began part IV by pointing to some shifts—not just in the history of how Tapalpa was founded but shifts in the whole genre of history—hence the many different strains of history, including the varieties that I had studied in Scotland, at Oxford, and at the University of Pennsylvania. There were also continuities in the history told of Tapalpa's founding, and I ended the previous chapter by noting that there were continuities and commonalities in the genre as well. Here I focus on the success of the genre of history in the Sierra but also far beyond. Why, more than a century after 1879, were people in the Sierra still talking about history? And how was it that in 1992 Tapalpans understood my questions about history and I understood their answers? How, in other words, has the genre of history been reproduced and disseminated across time and space? I have hinted at a few answers throughout the book and I bring them together in this chapter, which thus serves as a summary to the book. One of my answers is that history has been carried along with another success story—that of citizenship.

CHAPTER TEN

The Appeal of the Past

Not everyone need enthuse about history for the genre to prosper. I began part I by noting that some people, such as Federico in Atacco, were especially interested in history. Federico put work into persuading others of its worth, motivating them to talk and write history. But many others, starting with my landlady Teresa, were rather less interested in it. That bothered me because I was all fired up by my Oxford studies and keen to devote a year or two of my life to history. Yet many of the same people still valued the idea of history, offering a few tokens such as how Tapalpa was founded, even if they felt little inclined to talk any further. Similarly, I suspect that most British citizens learn little more than the idea of history and a few tokens that represent it—World War II, William the Conqueror, Oliver Cromwell, and the Virgin Queen. There are just enough enthusiasts to persuade people of history's value—including academics, fiction writers, organizers of local history associations, and armies of retired people who take history up as a hobby. And of course Stephen Fry, the British actor whom I mention in the preface.

What keeps the faithful few inspired by history? And what keeps others from dismissing it entirely? It is not easy to explain history's success. While gossip dwells on the immediate, history looks to a past that is anything but immediate. The past in Tapalpa made history boring or at least irrelevant. One solution was to spice up history with other genres such as legend, gossip or, indeed, fiction. Juan Rulfo did not mix his history with his fiction, but history in Britain has thrived as fiction—historical novels are regularly best sellers. Dramatized history, blended with romance, intrigue and glamor, has prospered at the box office and as prime-time viewing, no less so in Mexico with historical telenovelas such as *El Chacal* and *Soy tu dueña* (both set in haciendas).

Yet history's focus on the past is not just a burden—it gives history certain advantages over gossip. To begin with, while the past of history can be narrated as if it were over and done with, it can also be narrated as a step on the road to the present and future. Progress did feature in Tapalpa's history, as we have seen. Tapalpa progressed and overtook Atacco. So the past, where Atacco was the town, represented a step on the road to the present of Tapalpa being the town, even if for the most part people were happy simply to look back on Tapalpa's past. Mexican history was full of progress, crystallized in an independence that cast off the Spanish yoke and a Revolution that gave voice to social justice. National histories across the world are woven around a past that leads to the present (Dirks 1990). The British equivalent, although constantly "revised" by historians, was the past of monarchic tyranny leading, slowly but surely, to the democratic present.

I stressed in part I that pastness also makes the truth of history seem more objective, and therefore a good topic for public debate. In Tapalpa public debate was prized, even if little practiced. Juana gave up Fajardo's history classes, for example, because there was too much private gossip rather than public talk about the truth underlying legends. History as public debate is likewise prized in a book that I cited in my prologue: *Why History Matters*, by the British historian John Tosh (2008). The title of the book reminds us that history needs justifying—even academic historians feel the need to justify studying a past removed from the present. Tosh is wary of writing history with too much of an "eye on the present," and he worries about the crude ways in which people claim to "learn lessons from the past." Instead, Tosh points to a book by the American historians Joyce Appleby, Lynn Hunt, and Margaret Jacobs, *Telling the Truth about History* (1994), which defends the discipline by pointing to the "active debate" that it engenders, proposing that true democracy is less about voting than precisely about critical public debate. Tosh feels the need to advocate a more public role for British historians—they have been shy of bringing history to bear on public debates and on government policy. My undergraduate studies at Oxford made little mention of a public role, which is why I protested when Luis González y González began the master's degree program at El Colegio de Michoacán by insisting on the historian's "social duty." Historians have had a higher profile in Mexico than in Britain, as I noted in part III. But in both Britain and Mexico, the idea of history still gets reproduced with the idea of public debate, even if both history and public debate are often conspicuous by their absence.

Skewing and Anxiety

In part II I looked further into what Tapalpans got from history—if they were good at it—which also helps to explain why some were so keen on history. I started by homing in on the idea that places have their history. But I made it clear in the rest of part II that not everyone who tries can succeed at history, even to their own satisfaction. Knowing a place's history seems quite straightforward, especially if you are right there where it all in fact happened. That had lured Federico to attempt Atacco's history, as it has lured the legions of enthusiasts who take up family or local history elsewhere. But Federico had admitted: "we've seen that history is not good business." History was, I argued, skewed to people in other places. Documents were highly valued and yet often out of reach, while the know-how to make something of evidence close to hand, such as oral testimony, was often lacking. That may be less of an issue in Britain and in the United States, where there are greater resources for visiting archives, taking diploma courses, and so on. But many are still not in a position to produce authoritative history, and only recently have histories produced by the working class or ethnic minorities been taken seriously.

Does failure at history stymie history's success? On the contrary, the very difficulty of history makes successes all the more impressive, and reflected all the better on individuals like Fajardo, Arámbula, and Father Méndez, as well as on professionals like Fernández, Muriá, and González y González. There are also plenty of people who fail history exams at school yet go on to be avid readers of historical novels or films. The same is true of particular histories, which fall by the wayside without jeopardizing history itself. Much of the history that my father learned at school has now dropped out of the curriculum, much to his disgust, but history itself is still taught. In fact, anxiety is part of what keeps history (and histories) in circulation. Anxiety makes people worry about others challenging their history or even just asking them about it. It led Beto to memorize the first two paragraphs of my history just in case weekenders stopped by to ask. I noted that Mexican migrants in California were anxious about history because their rooting was in question, while chroniclers could be anxious about the academic historians who liked to criticize their "amateur" counterparts. Academics have anxieties of their own. The British anthropologist John Davis has written of the "professional relations of rivalry" that lead historians to challenge each other, although he suggests that such rivalry "sharpens their critical faculties" (Davis 1989, 115). I wonder whether the British public is as self-conscious as Mexicans are about their knowledge of history. Several commentators have complained of the U.K. citizenship test that most citizens by birth lack the knowledge of history that is expected of the applicants; but their complaint is less about citizens' ignorance of history and more just that the test is inappropriate.

I ended part II by noting that people looked elsewhere not just for evidence but for canons of evidence and the know-how to make something of it. That helps to explain why history has been reproduced so efficiently—why history had become so similar in Tapalpa and at Oxford. Instead of each place spawning its own kind of history, people around the world have received their understanding of history from central places. Oxford has been one of those central places, although not the only one and there have been shifts in the geography of historical knowledge. While at Oxford from 1988 to 1991, I was pointed to the work of French historians; at the University of Pennsylvania from 1995 to 2001, I was sometimes directed to the work of South Asian scholars in the subaltern studies tradition, although most were teaching at U.S. universities, which remain for now central places.

Investing in History

I began part III with what most scholars have focused on—the national history in which states across the world have invested. I suggested that the Mexican state has done a fine job of crafting a national history and getting people interested in it. Schooling, civic festivals, and radio and television have all played their part in disseminating the idea that nations are places that have history (Beezley and Lorey 2001). Tapalpans had certainly picked up on the idea and were as keen as anyone else to talk about Mexican history. Its powerful story of mestizaje and progress had even found its way into Tapalpa's history, despite the difference in kind between Tapalpa's and Mexico's histories.

History is older than the nation-state, though. In the New World it was already thriving during the centuries of Spanish colonial rule. The cultural historian Angel Rama (1984, 25) has written of the *letrados* (literally, lettered persons) who formed a kind of priestly caste of distinguished administrators in the Spanish colonies. Rama claims that this lettered caste governed over the countryside from the city—he describes them as the "lettered city" (32). Another cultural historian, Richard Kagan (2000, 135), argues that Creole letrados usually regarded their town or city as their *patria* (fatherland). Only later did Creoles begin to form alliances with their counterparts in other towns, seeking common cause against the native Spaniards favored by eighteenth-century Bourbon monarchs (Pagden 1987, 92–93). History was very much part of the repertoire of the letrados. Kagan has noted that many of these histories focused on the New World cities, giving the example of the Augustinian chronicler Antonio de la Calancha, who apologized that "his 'love' for his patria, the city of La Plata or Sucre, had led him to devote more pages to its history than that of other New World towns" (Kagan 2000, 130). That tradition was no stranger to west Mexico. As far back as 1742, a Guadalajaran lawyer had produced an authoritative history of the region (de la Mota y Escobar 1940 [1742]). I also mentioned in part II the nineteenth-century Sayulan lawyer, conversant in "Universal History," who was cited by Federico Munguía as an "illustrious son" of the town. His contemporaries González and Cedeño, the authors of the 1879 survey, were also heirs of the old tradition of letrados.

The Mexican state has done its best to nationalize the lettered city. After independence in 1821, it created a national bureaucracy and government officials liaised with the scribes or secretaries of provincial towns, who often developed a pivotal role (Rama 1984). For example, González and Cedeño wrote their 1879 survey at the behest of the state government of Jalisco. Schoolteachers joined the ranks of the letrados. The liberals in government from mid-nineteenth century were keen to introduce mass schooling, and González and Cedeño boasted of the modest public schools open in Tapalpa, although in fact most education remained in the Church's hands (Monroy 1956). Governments after the Revolution (1910–1917) went further in nationalizing the lettered elite. The century saw a massive expansion in government bureaucracy; the municipal government was required to produce regular plans and reports that often began with a section on Tapalpa's history. New schools were set up across the Sierra, including in rural communities; they were often poorly equipped and met with resistance, but were still significant in spreading literacy as well as bringing in more schoolteachers—I mentioned in part II the Guadalajaran schoolteacher who complained of Atacco's "cultural backwardness." The post-Revolutionary state undertook "Cultural Missions" into remote rural areas, which included Atacco (Lainé 1992). Further afield in the central Mexican state of Morelos, Friedlander observed that "villagers have been taught to feel indebted to outsiders for almost every 'improvement' they have acquired throughout their history, be it religion, land *or what is referred to in general as 'culture'"* (Friedlander 1975, 158; emphasis added).

Together with the "lettered city," the Mexican state attempted to nationalize the genre of history, just as nation-states have everywhere (Anderson 1991, 194–99). I have said that town chroniclers from the nineteenth century often tried to place their town in the context of national history, preferably giving it a significant role in that history. González and Cedeño portrayed Tapalpa as a victim of the endemic civil war, and one deserving of a respite.

They hedged their bets in terms of the political ideologies of the Jalisco state government, boasting of progress while also showing their respect for traditions and order. Mexican history was also taught in schools at that time, as González and Cedeño mention. The post-Revolutionary state did a more thorough job of nationalizing the genre of history, both by expanding schooling and by developing the rich pageant of nationalist festivals that I have described (Beezley and Lorey 2001; Lomnitz 2001; Pérez Siller and Radkau García 1998; Benjamin 2000). Government even tried, from the 1970s, to colonize what was told of local and regional history. I noted in part II that the Secretaría de *Cultura* had invested in "chronicler exchanges" across the region, and in part III I mentioned the appearance of regional history as a school subject, together with local history projects for pupils. That did push people to keep talking of Tapalpa's history—in case their children or grandchildren were asked for a project on the topic.

We have seen throughout the book, however, that the Mexican state has not been entirely successful in nationalizing history. We have noted the influence of Mexican history, with its ideas of progress and mestizaje, on Tapalpa's history, but also that Tapalpans did not often connect what they said of Mexican history with what they said of Tapalpan history. Even when asked to do projects on Tapalpa's history, most pupils simply lifted their projects word for word from books in the library; a valiant few interviewed the elderly but made little attempt to integrate the talk of the elderly with the national history of their school textbooks. One of the consequences was that national history did not undermine the history told of towns—and neither did the history of towns undermine national history. That was the difference between the history of towns and the "microhistory" of Luis González y González, which was pitched as a challenge to official Mexican history.

The nation-state was not, in any case, the only institution that invested in history. I showed in part II that the Tapalpan tourist industry has made its own investment in history and elsewhere tourism entrepreneurs have put time and money into it as well. Although Federico commented in Atacco that history is not always good business, it does seem to sell if it is dressed up in the right way. History for weekenders was made to seem homegrown, almost like the cryptic exoticism of legends. I have argued that it was as skewed as cosmopolitan history, just to a different set of expectations—those of weekenders in search of an idiosyncratic rural experience. I am not sure that rural tourism in the United Kingdom is much concerned with history—although an empty field where the Battle of Bannockburn was fought in 1314 receives busloads of visitors—but legend is certainly a selling point. As a child I visited one of the many Ossian's Caves in Scotland, on the Isle of Arran, and like many was briefly captivated by the enigmatic figure of Ossian, even though I learned nothing about him and, like Tapalpa's weekenders, never got around to asking. In California I found that the historical associations, although not commercial, dressed up history for residents and tourists, focusing their efforts more than in rural Mexico on the heritage of buildings, many of which dated back to the Californios from whom California had been taken (see illustration 29; Norkunas 1992; Handler and Gable 1997). Tourism is not the only market for history. I have mentioned its success in cinema and television, and a Tapalpan who had lived in San Francisco for much of his life told me that his newfound interest in family history was sparked by a CD that came with a bottle of Chivas Regal whisky. History sells on the internet too, although the several websites that feature Tapalpa's history, many geared to selling real estate in the Sierra, seem to have cut and pasted the same old history from the *Monograph of Tapalpa*.

We saw in part III that the Church, too, has invested in history. It sponsors not just accounts of saintly apparitions but also histories that I would call secular—that bracket God from the main flow of the narrative. Catholic priests were in a strong position to do secular history and it helped them shore up their authority, not least as second-class citizens. Indeed, many letrados were priests—the historian José María Muriá recalled a fierce fight

Illustration 29: Visitors being shown around an old house, run by a local historical association, in the vicinity of Concord, California (2008).

at the 1971 national conference of local historians, when the clergy finally lost control of that association. Father Méndez is an obvious example. Similarly, Oxford history kept its distance from established religion and few if any Oxford historians confess their devotion, even in the prologues to their academic books. Yet the Church of England was built into the very fabric of the university—chapels, quads, crosses, and gargoyles.

In Tandem with Citizenship

History has not made it on its own—it has been reproduced along with other things. Tosh (2008) links history to public debate, as I have said, and he goes on to argue that public debate is key to citizenship. Tosh refers back to the distinguished William Stubbs, the first Regius Professor of History at Oxford, who said in his inaugural lecture in 1867 that studying history could make for better citizens, not because of the information they acquired but because of the judgment that they cultivated. Stubbs went on to argue that the historian's faculty of judgment served not just for voting as a citizen but for tackling broader issues in life (Stubbs 1887).

I have shown that history has several links to citizenship. One of them is commitment to community. Tapalpans in California considered an interest in Tapalpa's history to be a sign of commitment to their town, while many Americans complain precisely that Mexicans remain committed to Mexico and should not be considered for U.S. citizenship (Hansen 2003). History can also be a sign of a good citizen. I have shown that history in Tapalpa gave people more of a voice in public life and even a cosmopolitan air. Fajardo, don Lupe, Arámbula, and Father Méndez were fine examples, each in their own way. Regionally, history gave a public voice to José María Muriá; nationally, to Héctor Aguilar Camín and Enrique Krauze. History helped to turn Stephen Fry from comic actor into public intellectual—still as amiable and at times caustic, but with a gravitas that is not all tongue-in-cheek. Tapalpans looked to history not just to show cultura but also to display their rooting to places. History had most to offer, I suggested, to men of learning and cultura, such as Arámbula, Fajardo, and Juan Rulfo, who were looking to root themselves back to their places of origin. I am tempted to add the actor Sean Connery, Scotland's most exotic exile and devotee of its history, to that list. History has much to offer, not just as a model of public debate but as a sign of a public persona.

Nation-states have invested in citizenship as well as in history, but I have argued throughout that neither was fully nationalized. Citizenship like history was urban in early modern Europe until states sought to roll out citizenship across national territory. However, the historian Tamar Herzog (2007) has argued that urban citizenship in Spain survived alongside national citizenship well into the nineteenth century, and perhaps into the twentieth century. She indicates, too, that the Spanish urban tradition, which included notions of citizenship, had been used as a template for colonization in the Americas. It is possible that urban citizenship survived the rise of national citizenship in Latin America as well (Hernández Chávez and Carmagnani 1997). Significantly, Claudio Lomnitz has argued that the formal extension of citizenship in Mexico was really a degrading of citizenship. Even after the Mexican Revolution, so-called "citizens" were not actually empowered to shape the future of their national community. He adds:

> Mexican political geography has recognized three to four main levels of political communities. Of these, the city, town, or village is the only political unit with an uninterrupted history of having matched government with the representation of a people and of a popular will. (Lomnitz 1995, 25)

Lomnitz does not identify this "uninterrupted history" as a tradition of urban citizenship, but it does help to explain my observation in the Sierra de Tapalpa that townspeople felt that they were citizens of towns and of the Mexican nation (Gordon and Stack 2007, 118). History and citizenship in the United Kingdom also have something of an association with towns and cities. There is no work of the stature of Luis González y González's *Pueblo en vilo* (1968), which had inspired me to start my project in Tapalpa, but there are many academic and non-academic histories of British towns and cities. I think, though, that both history and citizenship are less urban in the United Kingdom, even if my baby daughter received, along with her U.K. birth certificate, a certificate proclaiming her a "citizen of Aberdeen."

The Success of a Shifting History

I began part IV by looking at shifts in a particular history—the history of how Tapalpa was founded—and I went on to consider the success of that history. I also pointed to shifts in the genre of history and I believe they have helped to keep history fresh. History has been successful in the sense that some defining attributes, such as the idea of the past, have found their way far and wide. That is how I recognized as history what I was told in Tapalpa. But as history has gone in different geographical directions, it has gone in different generic directions—many new strains of history have emerged. Some strains are more successful than others. The tourist industry has whetted the appetite of millions for history-flavored travel, while local (and family) history is doing well among the growing numbers of retirees across the world, aided by how-to books, software tools, and websites. National history is perhaps starting to wane. Academic history is mainly national, which may explain the rush to justify "why history matters." But academic historians also keep trying to reinvent their discipline. Not only do particular histories get revised but historians champion new kinds of history, and history at the University of Pennsylvania in the mid-1990s sounded different from the University of Oxford history of the late 1980s. Their instinct serves them well—history is unlikely to survive by treading water.

No doubt the same is true of citizenship. Scholars have often tried to define citizenship for their own purposes, generally as membership in nation-states. But the success of citizenship is owed in part to its constant reinvention and repackaging. I have cited Lomnitz's account (1999) of the many reworkings of Mexican citizenship from independence up to the present day. Lomnitz insists that the idea of citizenship is reworked more often than the reality. The Mexican government has preferred to negotiate with power brokers of all sorts throughout Mexican territory, rather than follow the ideals of citizenship that it proclaims. In Britain, we were "subjects" until we were reclassified as "citizens" in 1981, citizenship has been taught as a school subject in England since the 1990s, and the U.K. government continues to surprise us with its schemes and programs for new and old citizens. It is far from clear in what sense, if any, we are more citizens than we were in 1981, but the idea of citizenship has certainly made it through the period and remains—in all its themes and variations—a lively item of public debate.

Epilogue

Citizenship Beyond the State?

I have argued that my informants in the Sierra de Tapalpa were citizens not just of Mexico but of their towns, and I suggested that their urban and national citizenships were different in kind. I have also indicated that some people were considered better citizens than others and that being a good citizen could result in a public voice. People considered to have cultura were, I have said, considered good citizens. I have shown, of course, that knowing history was closely linked to being citizens. Finally, I noted that Mexican citizenship had a secular edge (leaving priests as second-class citizens) although urban citizenship was less obviously secular.

Whereas my research from 1992 to 2005 focused on history with an eye on citizenship, my research since 2005 has focused on citizenship with an eye on civil society and rule of law (Stack 2012, 2010; Gordon and Stack 2007). I explained in part I that I have used "good or eminent citizens" for people who have acquired certain presence and standing in public life—a voice or authority in the town's affairs. When I asked in 2007 questions such as, "What does it mean to you to be a citizen?"—letting my informants make their own associations—I found that they did not always use the term in the same way as I have in the book. But they did not use it so differently, either, and I have noted that several offered as examples of citizenship the ways in which they participated in the life of their towns or cities. Every so often, moreover, an informant would bring up history in relation to what they considered citizenship. In part III I gave the example of Roberto, a small businessman in Zamora, who had said he felt like a citizen of Zamora as well as of Mexico and went straight on to compare Zamora and Mexico's histories, concluding that "the origin of the information is different."

Yet Roberto's response, which I quoted in full in part III, already takes us beyond the scope of this book. There is much more to say about citizenship. Roberto acknowledged government as a necessary evil, but complained about the dubious ideology of national heroes that it produces. Indeed, he viewed our relationship to government as not the essence of citizenship but a problem for it. Curiously, much of the academic literature on citizenship focuses precisely on government: how governments define citizenship and determine who gets to be citizens, and what citizens get in principle and in practice from government. This literature concentrates on rights and understands them narrowly as grounds for making claims on government. Social scientists have been chiefly concerned with how to turn rights on paper into the substantive exercise of rights. My informants, by contrast, talked about citizenship in much broader terms and did not reduce citizenship to a relationship with the state. For example, they spoke of fulfilling obligations to community as much as of claiming rights on the state, and also said that government merely authorized rather than granted citizenship. Some like Roberto talked of citizenship in terms of getting independence from the state. Similarly, I showed in part II that Andrés considered cultura to be an alternative route to politics, one that gave his group some room for maneuver beyond party politics.

Roberto went on to identify a third sense of citizenship. I asked whether it would sometimes be easier not to be a citizen, and he began his reply with the example of a trip that he had just taken with his family down to the coast. When you are travelling like that, he says, "you are passing by places and the problems are not yours." He agreed that you might lose some rights by not being a citizen, but that loss would be outweighed by being free of "a heap of obligations." Many interviewees followed suit by coupling rights and obligations or duties, and many did so stressing, like Roberto, that citizenship was not just about rights but about obligations as well. But Roberto ended up saying that citizenship is "a condition that you can't get rid of, wherever you are." He gave as an example his visits to the United States and to England, mainly to study. There, he tells us, he felt not just obligations but also made contributions, even just by purchasing clothes and food. In other words, Roberto began by considering citizenship as a kind of membership that one might shrug off but ended by thinking of it as an inescapable condition. He moved, in the process, from a modern, liberal position, focused on individual rights, to the Aristotelian ideal that has, like the urban traditions that I mention, refused to be occluded (Heater 1990; Dagger 1997). But I prefer to leave all that for my next book.

References

ARCHIVAL

ASRA: Archivo de la Secretaría de la Reforma Agraria, Delegación Guadalajara
APT: Archivo Parroquial de Tapalpa

PUBLISHED

Anderson, Benedict. 1991. *Imagined Communities: Reflections on the Origin and Spread of Nationalism.* London: Verso.

Appelbaum, Nancy P. 2003. *Muddied Waters: Race, Region, and Local History in Colombia, 1846–1948.* Durham, NC, and London: Duke University Press.

Appiah, Kwame Anthony. 1997. Cosmopolitan Patriots. *Critical Inquiry* 23 (3):617–39.

Appleby, Joyce, Lynn Hunt, and Margaret Jacob. 1994. *Telling the Truth about History.* New York: W. W. Norton.

Asad, Talal. 2003. *Formations of the Secular: Christianity, Islam, Modernity.* Palo Alto, CA: Stanford University Press.

Attwood, Bain. 2008. In the Age of Testimony: The Stolen Generations Narrative, "Distance," and Public History. In *The Public Life of History,* special issue of *Public Culture* 20(1):75–95.

Attwood, Bain, Claudio Lomnitz, and Dipesh Chakrabarty, eds. 2008. *The Public Life of History*, special issue of *Public Culture* 20(1):1–4.

Bakewell, Liza. 1995. *Bellas Artes* and *Artes Populares:* The Implications of Difference in the Mexico City Art World. In *Looking High and Looking Low: Art and Cultural Identity*, edited by Jo Bright and Liza Bakewell, 19–54. Tucson: University of Arizona Press.

Bakhtin, Mikhail. 1986. *The Problem of Speech Genres and Other Late Essays*. Austin: University of Texas Press.

Barry, Jonathan. 2000. Civility and Civic Culture in Early Modern England: The Meanings of Urban Freedom. In *Civil Histories: Essays Presented to Sir Keith Thomas*, edited by Peter Burke, Brian Howard Harrison, and Paul Slack, 181–96. Oxford: Oxford University Press.

Bartra, Roger. 1989. Changes in Political Culture: The Crisis of Nationalism. In *Mexico's Alternative Political Futures*, edited by Wayne A. Cornelius, Judith Gentleman, and Peter H. Smith, 65–92. San Diego: Center for U.S.-Mexican Studies, University of California.

Basso, Keith. 1996. *Wisdom Sits in Places: Landscape and Language Among the Western Apache*. Albuquerque: University of New Mexico Press.

Becerra, Celina Guadalupe, Maria Alicia Leo Loreto, María Guadalupe Jiménez, and Alejandro Solís Matías. 1997. *Jalisco Historia y Geografía*. México, D.F.: Editorial Limusa.

Beezley, William H., and David E. Lorey. 2001. *Viva Mexico! Viva la Independencia! Celebrations of September 16*. Wilmington, DE: Scholarly Resources.

Benjamin, Thomas. 2000. *La Revolución: Mexico's Great Revolution as Memory, Myth and History*. Austin: University of Texas Press.

Blommaert, Jan. 2004. Grassroots Historiography and the Problem of Voice: Tshibumba's Histoire du Zaïre. *Journal of Linguistic Anthropology* 14 (1):6–23.

Briggs, Charles L. 1992. Generic versus Metapragmatic Dimensions of Warao Narratives: Who Regiments Performance? In *Reflexive Language*, edited by John Lucy, 171–212. Cambridge: Cambridge University Press.

Butler, Matthew. 2005. *Popular Piety and Political Identity in Mexico's Cristero Rebellion: Michoacán, 1927–29*. Oxford: Oxford University Press for British Academy.

Camarena y Gutiérrez de Laríz, Gabriel de Jesús. 1987 (1879). Villa de Tapalpa. *Revista Jalisco* 8:20–52.

Carr, E. H. 1961. *What Is History?* New York: Vintage Books.

Certeau, Michel de. 1988. *The Writing of History*. Translated by T. Conley. New York: Columbia University Press.

Chafe, Wallace. 1986. Evidentiality in English Conversation and Academic Writing. In *Evidentiality: The Linguistic Coding of Epistemology*, edited by Wallace Chafe and Johanna Nichols, 261–272. Norwood, NJ: Ablex Publishing Corporation.

Chakrabarty, Dipesh. 1992. The Death of History? Historical Consciousness and the Culture of Late Capitalism. *Public Culture* 4 (2):47–65.

Colección de Acuerdos. 1868. *Colección de Acuerdos, Órdenes y Decretos de los Indígenas, Bienes de sus Comunidades y Fundos Legales de los Pueblos del Estado de Jalisco 3*. Guadalajara: Tipografía de J.M. Brambila.

———. 1879. *Colección de Acuerdos sobre Bienes de Indígenas y Fundos Legales 4*. Guadalajara: Tipografía de J. M. Brambila.

Craig, A. L. 1983. *The First Agraristas: An Oral History of a Mexican Agrarian Reform Movement*. Berkeley: University of California Press.

Dagger, Richard. 1997. *Civic Virtues: Rights, Citizenship and Republican Liberalism*. Oxford: Oxford University Press.

Davis, John. 1989. The Social Relations of the Production of History. In *History and Ethnicity*, edited by Elizabeth Tonkin, Maryon McDonald, and Malcolm Chapman, 104–20. London: Routledge.

de la Mota y Escobar, A. 1940 (1742). *Descripción geográfica de los reinos de la Nueva Galicia, Nueva Vizcaya y Nuevo León*. México, D. F.: Editorial Pedro Robedo.

de la Peña, Guillermo. 1980. Evolución Agrícola y Poder Regional en el Sur de Jalisco. *Revista Jalisco* 1:38–55.

———. 1992. Populism, Regional Power, and Political Mediation in Southern Jalisco 1900–1980. In *Mexican Regions*, edited by E. V. Young, 191–223. San Diego: University of California Press.

Dirks, Nicholas B. 1990. History as a Sign of the Modern. *Public Culture* 2(2):25–32.

Eidson, John. 2005. Between Heritage and Counter-Memory: Varieties of Historical Representation in a West German Community. *American Ethnologist* 32 (4):556–75.

Fabian, Johannes. 1990. *History from Below*. Amsterdam: John Benjamins.

Fahrmeir, Andreas. 2007. *Citizenship: The Rise and Fall of a Modern Concept*. New Haven, CT, and London: Yale University Press.

Fajardo Villavazo, José. 1994. Memoria sobre la devoción de San Antonio de Padua. *El Informador*, 11 June.

———. 1995. La Virgen de la Defensa. In *El Informador, Suplemento Cultural*, 17 December.

Feierman, Steven. 1990. *Peasant Intellectuals: Anthropology and History in Tanzania*. Madison: University of Wisconsin Press.

Fernández, Rodolfo. 2004. *Una Mirada a su Historia*. Guadalajar, Jalisco: Unión Editorialista.

Ferrarroti, Franco. 1990. *Time, Memory and Society*. Westport, CT: Greenwood Press.

Fitzgerald, Timothy. 2007. Introduction. In *The Secular-Religious Dichotomy: Historical and Colonial Contexts*, edited by Timothy Fitzgerald, 1–24. London: Equinox.

Friedlander, Judith. 1975. *Being Indian in Hueyapan: A Study of Forced Identity in Mexico*. New York: St. Martin's Press.

Fry, Stephen. 2006. The future's in the past. In *The Observer Review*, July 9.

González, Andrés. 1971 (1879). Estadística de la Municipalidad de Sayula. *Tzaulan*, May 9:3–4.

González y González, Luis. 1968. *Pueblo en vilo: microhistoria de San José de Gracia, Michoacán*. México, D. F.: El Colegio de México.

———. 1986. La Revolución Mexicana y los Revolucionados. *Nexos* 9:9–13.

González, Martín. 2002. *Defensora sin institución: Una interpretación histórica de la Virgen de la Defensa*. Atemajac de Brizuela, Jalisco: Parroquia de San Bartolomé Apóstol.

Gordon, Andrew, and Trevor Stack. 2007. Citizenship Beyond the State: Thinking with Early Modern Citizenship in the Contemporary World. In *Citizenship Beyond the State?*, special issue of *Citizenship Studies* 11(2), edited by Andrew Gordon and Trevor Stack, 117–33.

Halbwachs, Maurice. 1980. *The Collective Memory*. New York: Harper.

Handler, Richard, and Eric Gable. 1997. *The New History in an Old Museum*. Durham, NC, and London: Duke University Press.

Hanks, William. 1987. Discourse Genres in a Theory of Practice. *American Ethnologist* 14(4):668–92.

Hansen, Victor Davis. 2003. *Mexifornia: A State of Becoming*. Los Angeles, CA: Encounter.

Heater, Derek. 1990. *Citizenship: The Civic Ideal in World History, Politics and Education*. London and New York: Longman.

Hernández Chávez, Alicia, and Marcello Carmagnani. 1997. La ciudadanía orgánica mexicana, 1850–1910. In *Ciudadanía política y formación de las naciones. Perspectivas históricas de América Latina*, edited by Hilda Sábato, 371–404. México, D. F.: El Colegio de México y El Fondo de *Cultura* Económica.

Herzog, Tamar. 2007. Communities Becoming a Nation: Spain and Spanish America in the Wake of Modernity (and Thereafter). In *Citizenship Beyond the State?*, special issue of *Citizenship Studies* 11(2), edited by Andrew Gordon and Trevor Stack, 151–72.

Hobsbawm, Eric, and Terence Ranger, eds. 1983. *The Invention of Tradition*. Cambridge: Cambridge University Press.

Holston, James. 2008. *Insurgent Citizenship: Disjunctions of Democracy and Modernity in Brazil*. Princeton, NJ: Princeton University Press.

Holston, James, and Arjun Appadurai. 1999. Cities and Citizenship. In *Cities and Citizenship*, edited by James Holston, 1–18. Durham, NC, and London: Duke University Press.

The Home Office-Life in the UK Advisory Group. 2007. *Life in the United Kingdom: A Journey to Citizenship*. 2nd ed. London: TSO (The Stationery Office).

Hytner, Nicholas. 2006. *The History Boys*. Los Angeles, CA, and London: Fox Searchlight Pictures, DNA Films and BBC2 Films in association with National Theater.

Isin, Engin. 2007. city. state: critique of scalar thought. In *Citizenship Beyond the State?*, special issue of *Citizenship Studies* 11(2), edited by Andrew Gordon and Trevor Stack, 211–28.

James, Daniel. 2000. *Doña María's Story: Life History, Memory and Political Identity*. Durham, NC: Duke University Press.

Joutard, Philippe. 1986. *Esas voces que nos llegan del pasado*. Translated by N. Pasternac. México, D. F.: Fondo de *Cultura* Económica.

Kagan, Richard L. 1995. Clio and the Crown: Writing History in Hapsburg Spain. In *Spain, Europe, and the Atlantic World*, edited by Richard L. Kagan and Geoffrey Parker, 73–99. Cambridge: Cambridge University Press.

———. 2000. *Urban Images of the Hispanic World, 1493–1793*. New Haven, CT, and London: Yale University Press.

Klor de Alva, José de Jesús. 1992. Foreword. In *The Broken Spears: The Aztec Account of the Conquest of Mexico*, by Miguel León-Portilla. Boston, MA: Beacon Press.

Lainé, Cecilia Greaves. 1992. Proyectos y realidades de las misiones culturales (1942–1984). In *La ciudad y el campo en la historia de México: memoria de la VII Reunión de Historiadores Mexicanos y Norteamericanos*, 947–53. México, D. F.: Universidad Nacional Autónoma de México.

Lambek, Michael. 2003. "On Standing 'Outside' Religion: A View from the Pre-Alps," paper presented at American Anthropological Association annual meeting, November 2003.

Lazar, Sian. 2007. *El Alto, Rebel City: Self and Citizenship in Andean Bolivia*. Durham, NC: Duke University Press.

Linklater, Andrew. 1998. Cosmopolitan Citizenship. *Citizenship Studies* 2(1):23–41.

Lomnitz, Claudio. 1995. Ritual, Rumor and Corruption in the Constitution of Polity in Modern Mexico. In *Journal of Latin American Anthroplogy* 1(1):20–47.

———. 1999. Modes of Citizenship in Mexico. *Public Culture* 11(1), 269–94.

———. 2001. *Deep Mexico, Silent Mexico: An Anthropology of Nationalism*. Minneapolis: University of Minnesota Press.

———. 2008. Narrating the Neoliberal Moment: History, Journalism, Historicity. *Public Culture* 20(1), 39–56.

Low, Setha M. 1993. Cultural Meaning of the Plaza: The History of the Spanish-American Gridplan-Plaza Urban Design. In *The Cultural Meaning of Urban Space*, edited by Robert Rotenberg and Gary McDonogh, 75–98. Westport, CT: Bergin and Garvey.

Mallon, Florencia. 1995. *Peasant and Nation: The Making of Postcolonial Mexico and Peru*. Berkeley: University of California Press.

Marshall, Thomas. H. 2009 (1950). Citizenship and Social Class. In *Inequality and Society*, edited by Jeff Manzer and Michael Sauder. New York: W. W. Norton.

Méndez, Luis M. 1948. *Madre y Defensa*. Guadalajara, Jalisco.

———. 1989. Tapalpa, Tierra de Arriba. *Reflejos* 2, 6–17.

Meyer, Jean. 1971. *La Cristiada*. México, D. F.: Siglo XXI.

Mignolo, Walter. 2000. *Local Histories/Global Designs: Coloniality, Subaltern Knowledges, and Border Thinking*. Princeton, NJ: Princeton University Press.

Monroy, Guadalaupe. 1956. Instrucción pública. In *Historia moderna de México. Tomo II: La república restaurada. Vol. 2 La vida social*, edited by Daniel Cosío Villegas, 634–50. México, D. F.: Editorial Hermes.

Munguía Cárdenas, Federico. 1976. *La Provincia de Avalos*. Guadalajara, Jalisco: Departamento de Bellas Artes, Gobierno de Jalisco.

———. 1987. *Antecedentes y datos biográficos de Juan Rulfo*. Guadalajara, Jalisco: Gobierno de Jalisco.

Muriá, José María. 1995. *Historia y Geografia de Jalisco: Tercer Grado*. México, D. F.: Editorial Trillas.

———. 2003. *Nueve ensayos sobre historiografía regional*. México, D. F.: CONACULTA.

Nava López, José Guadalupe. 2002. Relatos de un pueblo mágico: su pasado, sus creencias, sus tradiciones. *Un rincón en la Sierra Tapalpa* 2, 5–6.

Nava López, José Guadalupe, María Patricia Nava Aguilar, María de Jesús Hernández de Huerta, Angélica Concepción Sánchez Vázquez, and Conrado Huerta Rodríguez. 1985. *Monografía de Tapalpa, Jalisco*. Tapalpa, Jalisco: Biblioteca Pública Municipal de Tapalpa.

Nora, Pierre. 1989. Between Memory and History: Les Lieux de Mémoire. *Representations* 26:7–25.

Norkunas, Martha K. 1992. *The Politics of Public Memory: Tourism, History, and Ethnicity in Monterey, California*. Albany: State University of New York Press.

Nugent, Daniel, and Ana Maria Alonso. 1994. Multiple Selective Traditions in Agrarian Reform and Agrarian Struggle: Popular Culture and State Formation in the Ejido of Namiquipa, Chihuahua. In *Everyday Forms of State Formation: Revolution and the Negotiation of Rule in Modern Mexico*, edited by Gilbert Joseph and Daniel Nugent, 209–46. Durham, NC: Duke University Press.

Orozco, Luis Enrique. 1954. *Iconografía Mariana de la Arquidiócesis de Guadalajara, Tomo 1*. Guadalajar, Jalisco: Arzobispado de Guadalajara.

Pagden, Anthony. 1987. Identity Formation in Spanish America. In *Colonial Identity in the Atlantic World, 1500–1800*, edited by Nicholas Canny and Anthony Pagden, 51–93. Princeton, NJ: Princeton University Press.

Palacios, Guillermo. 1999. Política cultural del estado posrevolucionario e identidad campesino-indígena. In *Bajo el signo del Estado*, edited by José Eduardo Zárate Hernández, 35–54. Zamora, Michoacán: El Colegio de Michoacán.

Pérez Siller, Javier, and Verena Radkau García, eds. 1998. *Identidad en el imaginario nacional: reescritura y enseñanza de la historia*. Puebla: Universidad Autónoma de Puebla, El Colegio de San Luis, Georg-Eckert-Institut.

Portelli, Alessandro. 1981. The peculiarities of oral history. *History Workshop Journal* 12(1):96–107.

———. 1998. Oral history as genre. In *Narrative and Genre*, edited by Mary Chamberlain and Paul Thompson, 23–45. London and New York: Routledge.

Rama, Angel. 1984. *La ciudad letrada*. Hanover, NH: Ediciones del Norte.

Redfield, Robert. 1941. *The Folk Culture of Yucatan*. Chicago: University of Chicago Press.

Rough Guide. 1994. South towards the coast: Tapalpa. Online document, http://hotwired.com/rough/mexico/central.states/jalisco/regions/chapala.html#tapalpa (accessed 1999).

Rulfo, Juan. 1986. *¿Dónde quedó nuestra historia? Hipótesis sobre historia regional* (Coleccion Rajuela 2). Colima: Escuela de Arquitectura, Universidad de Colima.

———. 1992. *Toda la obra*. México, D. F.: Archivos.

———. 1998 (1977). *Juan Rulfo (entrevista con Joaquín Soler Serrano)*. Madrid: Editrama.

Sacks, David Harris. 2007. Freedom to, Freedom from, Freedom of: Political Rights and Political Participation in Early Modern England. In *Citizenship Beyond the State?*, special issue of *Citizenship Studies* 11(2), edited by Andrew Gordon and Trevor Stack, 135–50.

Sassen, Saskia. 2002. The repositioning of citizenship: Emergent subjects and spaces for politics. *Berkeley Journal of Sociology* 46:4–25.

Sayles, John. 1996. *Lone Star*. Los Angeles, CA: Columbia Pictures.

Serrano, Javier. 2002. *La dimensión cultural de las remesas: Los tapalpenses y su comunidad transnacional*. Master's thesis. Guadalajara, Jalisco: Centro de Investigaciones y Estudios de Antropología Social-Occidente.

———. 2006. *El Sueño Mexicano: el retorno imaginado en las migraciones internacionales de Tapalpa y Tlacotalpan*. Doctoral Thesis. Guadalajara, Jalisco: Centro de Investigaciones y Estudios Superiores en Antropología Social-Occidente.

Stack, Trevor. 1994. *Historia del Templo de la Merced de Tapalpa, Jalisco*. Guadalajara, Jalisco: Imprenta Nueva Galicia.

———. 2006. The Skewing of History in Mexico. *American Ethnologist* 33 (3):427–43.

———. 2007(a). The Higher Ground: The Secular Knowledge of Objects of Religious Devotion. In *Religion and the Secular: Historical and Colonial Contexts*, edited by Timothy Fitzgerald, 47–70. London: Equinox.

———. 2007(b). Rooting and Cultura in West Mexico. *Bulletin of Latin American Research* 26 (3):399–418.

———. 2010. A Just Rule of Law? *Social Anthropology* 18 (3):346–55.

———. 2012, Beyond the state? Notions of citizenship in Mexico (and California). *Citizenship Studies* 16 (7).

Stephen, Lynn. 1997. Pro-Zapatista and Pro-PRI: Resolving the Contradictions of Zapatismo in Rural Oaxaca. *Latin American Research Review* 32 (2):41–70.

Stephen, Lynn, and Rosaria Pisa. 1998. Fractured hegemony: multiple interpretations of Zapatismo and agrarian policy in Oaxacan *ejidos*. In *Disputas por el México Rural*, edited by Sergio Zendejas and Peter de Vries, 125–64. Zamora, Michoacán: El Colegio de Michoacán.

Stubbs, William. 1887. *Seventeen Lectures on the Study of Medieval and Modern History*. Oxford: Clarendon Press.

Tapia Santamaria, José. 1986. Identidad social y religión en el Bajío Zamorano 1850–1900. El culto a la Purísima, un mito de fundación. *Relaciones: Estudios de Historia y Sociedad* 7(27):43–71.

Thomson, Alistair. 2006. Four Paradigm Transformations in Oral History. *The Oral History Review* 34 (1):49–70.

Tosh, John. 2008. *Why History Matters*. New York: Palgrave Macmillan.

Trouillot, Michel-Rolph. 1995. *Silencing the Past: Power and the Production of History*. Boston, MA: Beacon Press.

Tschida, John. 1991. Outside Guadalajara: The mountain village of Tapalpa. Online document, http://www.mexweb.com/reporter/reporter.htm#OUTSIDE (accessed 1999).

Turner, Bryan S. 2001. The Erosion of Citizenship. *British Journal of Sociology* 52 (2):189–209.

Un rincón en la Sierra Tapalpa. 2002. Atacco y sus curanderos. *Un rincón en la Sierra Tapalpa* 2, 11–13.

Urban, Greg. 2001. *Metaculture: How Culture Moves Through the World*. Minneapolis: University of Minnesota Press.

Uzeta, Jorge. 1997. El diablo y la santa. Imaginario religioso y cambio social en Santa Ana Pacueco, Guanajuato. Zamora, Michoacán: El Colegio de Michoacán.

Vanderwood, Paul. 1998. *The Power of Gods against the Guns of Government: Religious Upheaval in Mexico at the Turn of Nineteenth Century*. Palo Alto, CA: Stanford University Press.

Vasconcelos, José. 1979 (1925). *The Cosmic Race/La Raza Cósmica*. Translated by Didier T. Jaén. Baltimore, MD: Johns Hopkins University Press.

Vaughan, Mary Kay. 1997. *Cultural Politics in Revolution: Teachers, Peasants, and Schools in Mexico, 1930–1940*. Tucson: University of Arizona Press.

Verdery, Katherine. 1993. *National Ideology Under Socialism: Identity and Cultural Politics in Ceausescu's Romania*. Berkeley: University of California Press.

Walton, John. 1984. Culture and Economy in the Shaping of Urban Life: General Issues and Latin American Examples. In *The City in Cultural Context*, edited by John Agnew, John Mercer, and David Sopher, 76–93. Boston, MA: Allen & Ulwin.

Werbner, Pnina. 2006. Vernacular Cosmopolitanism. *Theory, Culture & Society* 23 (2–3):496–98.

White, Hayden. 1973. *Metahistory: The Historical Imagination in Nineteenth-Century Europe*. Baltimore, MD, and London: Johns Hopkins University Press.

———. 1987. *The Content of the Form*. Baltimore, MD: Johns Hopkins University Press.

Zárate Hernández, José Eduardo. 1997. *Procesos de Identidad y Globalización Económica: El Llano Grande en el Sur de Jalisco*. Zamora, Michoacán: El Colegio de Michoacán.

Index

academic historians: anxieties of, 138; conversations with, 13, 14, 19, 58, 59, 134, 137; debating value of history, xii, 22, 28–29, 137, 145; in Mexican institutions, 3, 57, 58–59, 74, 85, 88, 89, 90, 105, 123, 137, 143; relations with municipal chroniclers, 59, 89; writing microhistory, 3, 33, 59, 85, 141; of region, xv, 3, 7–8, 58, 59. *See also* El Colegio de Jalisco; El Colegio de Michoacán; González y González, Luis; history; Muriá, José María; oral history; Oxford history; University of Pennsylvania; written history

anthropology, 17; as opposed to history, 14, 19, 29; of history, xiii–xiv, 14–15. *See also* methodology; perceptions of researcher by informants

antiquity of settlements: disputes about, 50, 52, 116, 132; relative to other settlements, 11–12, 41–42, 113–14, 121, 125, 126–34. *See also* civic status of settlements; founding of towns; indigenous people or Indians

anxiety about knowing history, 52, 62, 66–67, 71, 138. *See also* authority to tell history

Apache, comparison with, 53–54

Appiah, Kwame Anthony, 62, 78

archaeology and archaeological remains, 21, 42–43, 49–50, 63, 68, 75, 83. *See also* pre-Hispanic

architecture. *See* buildings and settlement layout

archives: church, 56, 106, 114; findings in, 12, 56, 114, 126; creating own, 51, 57; distance and access to, 47–48, 51, 54, 55–56, 57, 106, 114, 138; municipal, 55, 127; value attributed to, 43, 51, 74. *See also* documents

Atemajac, 16, 97, 102

authenticity: of documents, 58 (*see also* truth of history); of tourism destinations, 66, 141 (*see also* tourism: rustic [*típico*] as tourist image)

authority that derives from knowing history, xii, 15, 17, 138–39; from producing secular history, 104, 105–7; as sign of *cultura*, 44–45, 57, 123 (see also *cultura* [cultivation]); marking as good or eminent citizens, xii, 17, 29, 45, 54, 59, 75, 95, 123, 136, 143–44 (*see also* citizenship and history). *See also* authority to tell history; history

authority to tell history: allowing to shape others' histories, 112, 117, 120–21, 128; deferring to someone with, 20, 55, 57, 64

161

162   INDEX

64–65, 117; from studying history, 57, 131; lack of, 48, 52, 54, 81, 88, 138; to produce full-fledged history, 15, 29–30, 44, 52, 54, 62, 63, 65, 75; to produce or challenge national history, 81, 88; shown by confidence, 29, 30, 55, 57. *See also* anxiety about knowing history; authority that derives from knowing history; challenging others' histories; history

belonging. *See* rooting (*arraigo*)
buildings and settlement layout, 11–12, 37, 39, 48–50, 66, 69–70, 120, 129. *See also* Church, Catholic: buildings; plaza; urban

California, fieldwork in, xii, xiii, xiv, 21, 71–73, 134, 142. *See also* migration: to California and other U.S. destinations; U.S., comparison to
Catholicism. *See* Church, Catholic
challenging others' histories, 45, 54, 59, 74–75, 81–92 passim, 101, 131, 138, 141. *See also* authority to tell history; official history: scepticism about
children. *See* young people and children
chroniclers, municipal: beyond Tapalpa, 56, 57–58, 59, 75, 140, 141; of Tapalpa, 21, 25, 26–27, 56–59, 75, 104; relations with academic historians, 59, 89
Church, Catholic: archdiocese of Guadalajara, 98; buildings, 5, 43, 49, 55, 95, 98, 100–101, 104, 114–15; churchyards, 36, 37, 49; conservative Catholicism, xv; diocese of Ciudad Guzmán, 35, 98, 102, 104; lay leaders, 101–3, 104, 106; liberation theology, 35, 102–3, 104; role in education, 140; sponsoring or publishing history, 98, 101–3, 104, 123–24, 142–43; traditional Catholicism, 106. *See also* festivals (fiestas): church-related; priests
cities, xiv. *See also* Ciudad Guzmán; civic status of settlements: town as opposed to city; Guadalajara; history of towns and cities; migration: to Guadalajara and other cities; urban

citing sources and giving credit, 27, 44–45, 52. *See also* copying from other histories and documents; evidence for history
citizenship: broader views of, xiv, 17–18, 45–46, 77–78, 147–49; local understandings of, 18, 45–46, 90–94, 147; as membership of community, 77–78, 143 (*see also* rooting [*arraigo*]); of priests, 95, 103–4, 106–7; relation to government, 46; shifts in, 145; tests, xii, 61, 138. *See also* authority that derives from knowing history; citizenship and history; cosmopolitan: citizens; *cultura* (cultivation); good or eminent citizens; rights; urban citizenship, as opposed to national
citizenship and history, xii, 34, 45, 59, 90, 123, 135, 143–44, 148. *See also* citizenship; history
Ciudad Guzmán, 9–10, 35, 56–57, 101–2, 104, 123–24
civic status of settlements: municipal agency as opposed to delegation, 37–38, 52–53; town as opposed to city, 66–70; town as opposed to hacienda, 11, 113, 120–22; town as opposed to villa, 126; town as opposed to village, 12, 29, 34, 37, 39, 43, 128. *See also* antiquity of settlements; cities; *cultura* (cultivation): in towns and cities; history of towns and cities; urban: as opposed to rural; villages
civility and civic virtue, 34, 40, 45, 77. *See also cultura* (cultivation)
Colegio de Jalisco, El (research center), 57, 58–59
Colegio de Michoacán, El (research center), 3, 13, 105, 137
Colima, state of, 57, 63, 74–75, 76
colonial period: as context, 125, 139–40, 144; references to, 23, 49, 51, 55, 58n, 68, 82. *See also* Conquest, Spanish
community, 36–37, 45–46, 78, 148. *See also* indigenous peoples or Indians: indigenous community; lands: loss of community

INDEX

Conquest, Spanish, 51, 82, 100, 103, 113, 117, 130
copying from other histories and documents, 57, 59, 98–99, 130, 141, 142. *See also* citing sources and giving credit
core and periphery: ethnic, 118–20; of settlements, 69–70, 118–20. *See also* buildings and settlement layout; ethnicity
cosmopolitan: citizens, 29, 62, 74–77, 143; *cultura*, 29, 62; knowledge, 45, 57, 62, 63–64, 106–7; tension with belonging, xiv, 62. See also *cultura* (cultivation); illustrious sons (*hijos ilustres*); rooting and *cultura*, relation of
Creoles and Spaniards, 58, 113, 116–19, 129, 139
Cristeros, xv, 3; arguments about, 57; opposing land reform, 12; relation to Mexican Revolution, 84, 85, 88; in Sierra de Tapalpa, 7, 9–10, 55, 85, 119; specific events reported, 55, 57
cultura (cultivation), 29; Cultural Missions, 37, 140; loss of, 63; as opposed to politics, 36–38, 55, 148; and secular history, 105–6; shown in knowing history, 44–45, 55, 57, 62, 63, 123; as sign of good citizen, 45–46, 55, 58; those held to have, 37, 40, 55, 64, 73, 74–76; those held to lack, 37, 40, 55, 65–68, 73; in towns and cities, 34, 37, 38, 40, 65, 68, 75, 123. *See also* cosmopolitan: *cultura*; illustrious sons (*hijos ilustres*); rooting and *cultura*, relation of
Cultural Missions, 37, 140

dates, 51, 67, 86, 87, 91
documents: authority of, 58; author's use of, 112–13, 114, 115–16, 126–27; difficulty in interpreting, 51, 58, 138; as index of town's civic status, 43; legal as opposed to historical, 23, 127–28; making own archive, 43, 48, 51; political or economic uses of, 44–45; (supposed) lack of, 6, 49, 55; use in written histories, 58, 59, 98, 117, 130, 133; as valued evidence for history, 34, 43, 47, 138. *See also* archives; citing sources and giving credit; copying other histories and documents; lands: land titles and related documents; legal discourse

economy, 69, 70, 71, 72, 113, 126; agriculture and forestry, 4, 16; crisis, 7; economic rationale for migration, 71, 72n; effect of tourism on housing, 69–70; employment and occupation, 10, 16, 35; government and NGO projects, 16, 35; industrial and mining, 7, 113, 126–27. *See also* elite families; interests, economic or political; lands; migration; tourism
education and schools: adult literacy teaching, 37; autodidacts, 57; building of schools, 7, 13, 140; Church's role in, 140; closing of municipal schools, 6, 119; Cultural Missions, 37, 140; Education Ministry, 8, 119; migrating to study, 71, 75; people's lack of, 16, 35, 50; in relation to *cultura*, 45; secularization of, 104, 140; seminary, 106; universities, 68, 70 (*see also under* academic historians). *See also* schoolteachers; teaching of history
ejidos (agrarian collectives): ejido members criticized, 85; process of founding, 8, 12–13, 116, 119; politics of, 13, 38; pride in Mexican Revolution, 88; selling of use rights, 15–16; sidelining of non-ejido members, 36. *See also* lands: land reform
elderly people as source of history, 4–5, 6, 11–12, 22, 29, 43, 48, 50, 62, 65, 71, 86, 97–98, 123, 132, 141, 145
elite families: in centre of towns, 12, 50, 64, 132; during revolution, 6; as employers, 12, 16, 50, 132; influence on politics, 13; as landowners, 7–8, 12, 13, 23–24, 111–12, 119, 132; links to hacienda, 120–21; migration of, 6, 8, 10; as old or most obviously rooted, 64, 111–12, 116–17, 120, 132; shaping history, 120, 126–27, 128, 132
ethnicity, xv, 117–19, 129, 133, 138. *See also* Creoles and Spaniards; indigenous people or Indians; *mestizaje*; protagonists of history

evidence for history, xiii, 23, 27, 34, 43, 47–59 passim, 63, 114, 120, 130–31, 134, 138–39. *See also* archaeology and archaeological remains; documents; oral history; written history

family: family histories, 33, 75, 116, 138, 142; as opposed to public, 7, 22, 25, 39; as source of history, 91–93, 116, 128, 132. *See also* elite families

festivals (fiestas): church-related, 35, 37, 52, 72, 95, 97–98, 100, 104; national, 37, 83, 87, 92, 141. *See also* Church, Catholic; nationalism and patriotism; parades

fiction: fictionalised history, 136; as opposed to history, 77. *See also* Rulfo, Juan

films and television: about historical knowledge, 27, 29; historical, 24, 123, 136; telenovelas, 24, 136; video recording, 72, 103. *See also* new media

founding of towns, 11, 20, 41, 51, 100, 111–22 passim, 125–34 passim. *See also* antiquity of settlements; civic status of settlements

full-fledged history: as definitive account, 54; as opposed to mere knowledge of the past, 62–70 passim, 74; as opposed to sources, 52; as opposed to traces or remains, 44. *See also* authority to tell history: to produce full-fledged history

genre, history as, xiv, 43, 47, 48, 112, 134, 135, 140

González y González, Luis, 3, 33, 59, 85, 88, 89, 90, 123, 137, 141, 144

good or eminent citizens, xii, 17–18, 29, 45, 54, 58, 59, 89, 95, 105–7, 147. *See also* authority that derives from knowing history; citizenship

gossip (chisme), as opposed to history, 19–20, 22, 25–27, 136

government or state: citizens' independence from, 36, 37, 46, 57, 85, 89, 148; federal 8–9, 12, 37, 38, 76–77, 89, 90, 91, 112, 119, 139–40, 145; influence on history, 112, 119, 122, 123, 139; Jalisco state, 8, 56, 57, 126, 140, 141; municipal, 13, 38, 40, 41, 45–46, 52–53, 59, 115–16, 131, 132, 140; post-Revolutionary, 9, 12, 112, 122, 126, 128, 140–41. *See also* education and schools; municipal presidents (or mayors); nationalism and patriotism; politics

Guadalajara, 4, 10, 16, 35, 55–56, 57, 59, 65–71, 75, 105. *See also* migration: to Guadalajara and other cities; tourism; weekenders

haciendas: beyond Tapalpa, 72, 122; buildings, 120, 122; as civic status of settlement, 11, 113, 121; elite families linking to, 120–21; as glamourous, 122, 136; in history told of Tapalpa, 11, 114–16, 118, 120–22, 129; owners, 85, 105, 114–15, 116; state propaganda about, 120. *See also under* lands

hierarchy and inequality. *See* authority that derives from knowing history; civic status of settlements; elite families; ethnicity

historians. *See* academic historians; authority to tell history; chroniclers, municipal; Oxford history

history: as bonito or harmless, 10, 25; commercial appeal of, 89, 141, 142; conservative nature of, 25, 29; difficulties in knowing, 47–59; evaluation of one's own or someone else's, 15, 48; know-how to produce, 48, 54, 114, 138; lessons of, 24, 83, 85, 137; potted or consensual, 24, 34, 66–67, 111, 112, 126, 133; tokens of, 133, 136; told by victors rather than vanquished, 24; versions of, 14, 55, 111. *See also* academic historians; authority that derives from knowing history; authority to tell history; citizenship and history; evidence for history; full-fledged history; genre, history as; history of towns and cities; microhistory; national history; oral history; Oxford history; public; written history

history of towns and cities: beyond Sierra de Tapalpa, 122, 133, 134, 144; in relation to national history, xii, 15, 33, 81, 123, 139–40; as sign of a town or city, 15, 29, 34, 40–46 passim, 123. *See also* history; urban citizenship, as opposed to national

identity. *See* rooting (*arraigo*)

illustrious sons (*hijos ilustres*), 62, 75–77, 84, 140. *See also* cosmopolitan: citizens; rooting and *cultura*, relation of

indigenous people or Indians: as backward or wayward, 35, 98–99, 129, 131; indigenous communities, 23–24, 36, 114–16, 128, 130; as protagonists in history of towns, 72, 100, 105, 111, 113–20, 129. *See also* antiquity of settlements; ethnicity; pre-Hispanic

intellectuals, 15, 89, 139–40. *See also* academic historians; chroniclers, municipal; *letrados* (lettered elite)

interests, economic or political, 14, 39–40, 44–45, 84, 111, 125, 126–28, 132. *See also* public: good or interest

Jalisco, state of, 27, 58–59, 74, 75, 76, 90, 123, 140, 141; southern Jalisco, region of, 7–8, 13, 29

Juanacatlán, 16, 95, 96, 97–98, 106, 129

lands: land disputes, 10, 12, 23–24, 36, 51, 53, 105, 115–16, 120; land reform, 8–10, 12, 85, 116, 119, 120, 127; land titles and related documents, 23–24, 58, 120, 127–28; loss of community, 12, 23–24, 105, 115–16, 127. *See also ejidos*; elite families: as landowners; haciendas

lawyers, 26–27, 55–56, 70, 74, 75

legal discourse, 15–16, 23–24, 51. *See also under* lands; documents

legends, as opposed to history, 21–22, 25–26, 41–43, 67, 68, 142

letrados (lettered elite), 34, 139–40. *See also* chroniclers; *cultura* (cultivation); intellectuals

libraries, 7, 23, 37, 43, 51, 56, 77, 100, 141. *See also* archives

media. *See* films and television; new media; newspapers and magazines

memory, individual and collective, xiii, 14, 65, 71; history as memory as opposed to knowledge, 15

mestizaje (racial or cultural mixing), 88, 117–19. *See also* ethnicity

methodology, xiii, xiv–xv, 6–7, 16–18, 114, 147–48. *See also* anthropology; perceptions of researcher by informants

Mexico. *See* national history; nationalism and patriotism; urban citizenship, as opposed to national

Michoacán, state of, 49, 68, 74, 84, 85, 91, 105, 148

microhistory, 3, 33, 59, 85, 141. *See also* academic historians; history; history of towns and cities

migrants' interest in and knowledge of history, xii; disavowal of interest in California history, 72; historical knowledge expected of migrants, 61, 62, 70–73; interest in hometown history by migrants, 62, 71–72. *See also* history; migration

migration, 61–62, 130; from Atacco to Tapalpa, 41, 50, 64, 118, 120; to California and other U.S. destinations, 4, 10, 14, 16, 63, 70–73, 143; complicating membership in community, 78; of cosmopolitans, 62, 70 (*see also* illustrious sons [*hijos ilustres*]); from elsewhere to Tapalpa, 116, 117; to Guadalajara and other cities, 4, 9, 16, 70; prejudice against migrants, 63, 71, 72n, 143; return visits to Tapalpa, 55, 70, 103, 117; from villages to towns, 5, 10, 16, 113. *See also* migrants' interest in and knowledge of history; rooting (*arraigo*); rooting and *cultura*, relation of

modernity and progress: backward or lacking in, 35, 66, 127, 131; in history, 113, 136; moral tales or stories, 53–54; signs of, 119–20, 126–27, 129, 140–41

municipal presidents (or mayors): actions of, 13, 56, 85, 131; celebrating Independence, 83; connections to, 56; discrimination at hands of, 40, 64, 68, 131; evaluation of, 40, 55, 64, 129; meeting with, 41, 45–46; privileges of, 55. *See also* government or state: municipal; politics

Muriá, José María, 58–59, 76, 82, 84, 89, 90, 123, 142, 143

museums, 83, 85

national citizenship. *See* urban citizenship, as opposed to national

national history, xii, 15, 36, 37, 81–93 passim, 136–37, 139; heroes, 82, 83, 84, 86, 87, 88–89, 91, 148; nationalizing history, 140–41. *See also* festivals (fiestas): national; history; history of towns and cities; nationalism and patriotism; official history; parades; teaching of history

nationalism and patriotism, 46, 71, 75, 81, 91, 92. *See also* urban citizenship, as opposed to national

new media, 142, 145

newspapers and magazines, 52, 55, 56, 58, 66, 89, 112–13, 122. *See also* written history

official history, 81, 82, 85, 141; as centralist, 84, 90; scepticism about, 82, 88, 92–93

old families. *See* elite families

old towns. *See* antiquity of settlements

oral history: academic oral history, 13–14, 17, 28, 134; collecting oral accounts, 7, 9–10, 50, 117, 141; disparities between oral and written accounts, 130–31, 141; oral accounts as alternative to written sources, 6, 114, 117; oral accounts as ultimately for writing, 17. *See also* history; written history

outsiders or people not "from here": bringing *cultura*, 140; challenging town's history, 45; interest in town's history, 23, 44, 50, 61, 129; knowing more about town's history, 72; sidelining of, 40, 61, 64, 78. *See also* rooting (*arraigo*)

Oxford history, 14, 19, 20, 24, 27, 47–48, 134, 137, 139, 143, 145. *See also* academic historians; history; U.K., comparison to

parades, 83–84, 90. *See also* festivals (fiestas): national

past, idea of the, xiii, 19–29, 45, 52, 136–37, 145. *See also* history

perceptions of researcher by informants, 5, 10, 17, 21–22, 29, 47–48, 57, 72, 101; evaluation of attempts to write history, 10, 33, 67. *See also* methodology

periphery. *See* core and periphery

places: and association with history, 15, 43; as objects of knowledge 48, 53, 62. *See also under* history of towns and cities

plaza (town or city square), 12–13, 37, 43, 49, 50, 69, 95. *See also* buildings and settlement layout

political parties, 36; PAN (National Action Party), 56; PRI (Revolutionary Institutional Party), 86, 119, 131. *See also* politics

politics, 55; connections in, 90; municipal, 10, 40, 57; national, 90; sidelining from, 40; staying out of, 57–58. *See also cultura* (cultivation): as opposed to politics; government or state; municipal presidents

postcolonial approaches, xi, xiv, 28–29, 47, 62, 139

poststructuralist approaches, xiii–iv, 28–29, 34, 99, 134

pre-Hispanic, 49–50, 68, 69, 74, 82–83, 84. *See also* archaeology and archaeological remains

priests, 91, 97–99, 103–4, 106–7, 142–43; as authorities on history, 56, 70, 75, 95, 98–99, 104, 106–7, 117. *See also* Church, Catholic

progress. *See* modernity and progress

protagonists of history: Creoles and Spaniards, 58, 113–20; divine as opposed to human, 94–105 passim; indigenous people or Indians, 72, 100, 105, 113–20; priests, 98. *See also* national history: heroes

public: debate, xii, 26, 39, 45, 47, 91, 137, 143; good or interest, 40; knowledge, xiii, 25, 45; role or duty of historian, 137; spirit

36–37, 40, 44–46. *See also* family: as opposed to public; interests, economic or political
pueblos (towns). *See* under history of towns and cities; civic status of settlements; urban citizenship, as opposed to national

ranchos (villages). *See* villages (ranchos)
regional history and historians, 7–10, 57, 58n, 59, 74–77, 81–82, 84; as school subject, 88, 90. *See also* Jalisco, state of; teaching of history: diploma in regional history
religion. *See* Church, Catholic
retirees, 10, 145. *See also* elderly people as source of history
revolutions: as context, 6, 8, 24, 119, 122; talk and writing about, 82, 84–87, 136. *See also* Cristeros; government or state: post-Revolutionary
rights, 8, 17, 34, 45, 82, 95, 148–49
rooting (*arraigo*): as antidote to emigration, 61, 73; degrees of rooting, 62, 64, 73; from knowing history, 14, 24, 61, 64, 65, 67; lack of, 14, 61–62, 63, 73; to Mexico, 91; of migrants, 71; to multiple places, 73, 74; relation to citizenship, 77–78, 91; sidelining of those not "from here," 40, 61, 64, 78. *See also* elite families: as old or most obviously rooted; migration; outsiders; tourism: rustic (*típico*) as tourist image
rooting and *cultura*, relation of: those who balance rooting and *cultura*, 62; those with *cultura* trying to claim rooting, 74–77, 78; those with rooting but not *cultura*, 62, 65–69; weekenders who try to juggle rooting and *cultura*, 68–69. *See also* cosmopolitan: citizens; *cultura* (cultivation); illustrious sons (*hijos ilustres*); rooting and *cultura*
Rulfo, Juan, 14, 57, 62, 67, 69, 74–77, 78, 81–82, 143
rustic (*típico*). *See* under tourism

schools. *See* education and schools; schoolteachers; teaching of history

schoolteachers, 35, 71, 82, 83, 84, 88, 105, 140. *See also* education and schools; teaching of history
secular history, debates about, 94, 99, 103; secularizing history, 98
secularism, political, 99–100, 103–4, 105–6, 147
settlement layout. *See* buildings and settlement layout
Sierra del Tigre, 84, 116–17
skewing of history, 47–59, 88, 112, 128, 132–33, 137–39, 141
Spaniards. *See* Creoles and Spaniards
state. *See* government or state; politics
streets, naming of, 36, 85, 90. *See also* buildings and settlement layout
sources. *See* evidence for history

talks and lectures on history, 56, 62, 67
teaching of history, 21, 24, 27, 29, 82–90 passim, 91–92, 125, 139, 141; diploma in regional history, 21–22, 24, 26–27, 57, 58, 59, 123; history textbooks, 55, 82, 83, 88–89, 119, 141; regional history as school subject, 52, 88, 90; school projects on Tapalpa, 24, 52, 88, 99, 129, 141. *See also* education and schools; schoolteachers
telenovelas, 24, 136. *See also* films and television
textbooks. *See* teaching of history
tourism: development of, 4, 10, 16; difficulties in fitting tourist image, 67–68, 69–70; use of history to promote, 141; lack of in Atacco, 35, 41; rustic (*típico*) as tourist image, 66–70, 123, 141; status of *Pueblo Mágico* (Magical Town), 16; as source of income and employment, 10. *See also* weekenders
towns (pueblos). *See* under history of towns and cities; civic status of settlements; urban citizenship, as opposed to national
tradition and customs, 36, 100, 114, 126, 133, 141
truth of history, 22, 25–26; criteria of, 55; as definitive accounts, 54; in history for weekenders, 67–68; of national history,

81, 82, 91; as objectivity, 28–29; as "what in fact happened," 20–25. *See also* full-fledged history; history

U.K., comparison to, xii, 3, 21, 27, 34, 61, 134, 136–45 passim. *See also* Oxford history
universities. *See under* academic historians; education and schools
University of Pennsylvania, 139, 145
urban: improvement, 52; as opposed to rural, xv (*see also* tourism: rustic [*típico*] as tourist image); services, 12–13, 41, 45–46, 82. *See also* buildings and settlement layout; civic status of settlements; plaza; urban citizenship, as opposed to national
urban citizenship, as opposed to national: academic debates on, xiv, 18, 34, 82; comparisons with U.K., 34, 144; difference in kind between, 82, 90–93; link to Latin American urban cosmopolitanism, 34, 139–40; local understandings of, 46, 90, 147–48; nationalization of citizenship, 144; secularism of urban and national, 105. *See also* citizenship; nationalism and patriotism
urban history. *See* history of towns and cities
U.S., comparison to, 29, 138, 143. *See also* California, fieldwork in; University of Pennsylvania

value of or interest in history, xiii, 24, 63; among migrants, 62; among weekenders, 66–67; encouraged by schools, 87, 123, 141; lack of, 10, 19–20, 24, 52, 59, 66–67, 136; as sign of *cultura*, 44–45; those who valued highly, xi, 11–12, 136; value given to truth of history, 20–30 passim, 137. *See also* academic historians: debating value of history; education and schools; truth of history
villages (ranchos), 9, 39–40, 69. *See also* civic status of settlements: town as opposed to village; urban: as opposed to rural
virgins and saints: cult of, 92, 95; history of, 25, 94–107 passim; miracles by, 95, 96–97, 102–3. *See also* Church, Catholic; festivals (fiestas): Church related

weekenders, 4, 16; asking questions about history, 52, 66–67 (*see also* anxiety about knowing history); expecting only rustic history, 62, 65; who juggle rooting and *cultura*, 68–69. *See also* outsiders; tourism
west Mexico as region, xv, 75, 85
written history, 33, 44; belief that book existed, 27n, 65; drawing on oral accounts in written history, 123, 130, 133, 134; drawing on written history in oral accounts, 123, 130; leaflets and printed sheets, 17, 52, 67, 68, 96; newspaper or magazine articles, 17, 56; oral accounts as ultimately for writing, 17; published non-academic books, 17, 56, 57, 59, 67, 69, 75–76, 98, 101–3, 117; unpublished monographs, 75, 77, 84, 99–100, 129; within bureaucratic documents, 99. *See also under* academic historians; documents

young people and children, 20–21, 24, 57, 71, 72, 84, 92, 96. *See also* education and schools; teaching of history

www.ingramcontent.com/pod-product-compliance
Lightning Source LLC
Chambersburg PA
CBHW021843220426
43663CB00005B/378